1 0 0 % B E R L I N

1 0 0 % B E R L I N

There's so much to experience in Berlin; where do you start? Of course you'll want to visit Alexanderplatz, Brandenburg Gate and the remains of the Wall. But also be sure to shop till you drop on Alte Schönhauser Strasse, discover nice restaurants and bars on Kollwitzplatz, climb up the Siegessäule for a great view over the city and get a taste of Turkish Berlin in Kreuzberg. This guide will take you everywhere you want to go in no time at all - sight-seeing, shopping, culinary delights and adventure - and easy-to-use maps will show you the way.

100% BERLIN, EXPLORE THE CITY IN NO-TIME!

Contents

100% Easy-to-Use

To make this guidebook easy-to-use, we've divided Berlin up into six neighbor-hoods and provided a detailed map for each of these areas. You can see where each of the neighborhoods lies in relation to the others on the general map in the front of the book. The letters Ⓐ to Ⓨ will also let you know where to find attractions in the suburbs, hotels, and nightclubs, all descri-bed in detail later on in the guidebook.

In the six chapters that follow, you'll find detailed descriptions of what there is to do in the neighborhood, what the area's main attractions are, and where you can enjoy good food and drink, go shopping, take a walk, or just be lazy. All addresses have a number ①, and you'll find these numbers on the map at the end of each neighborhood's chapter. You can see what sort of address the number is and also where you can find the description by looking at its color:

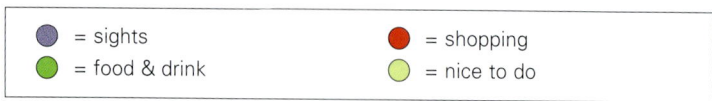

- ● = sights
- ● = food & drink
- ● = shopping
- ● = nice to do

6 WALKS

Every chapter also has its own walk, and the maps all have a line showing you the walking route. The walk is described on the page next to the map, and it will take you past all of the most interesting spots and best places to visit in the neighborhood. You won't miss a thing. Not only will you see the most important sights, museums, and parks, but also special little shops, good places to grab lunch, and fantastic restaurants for dinner. If you don't feel like sticking to the route, you'll be able to find your way around easily with the descriptions and detailed maps.

PRICE INDICATION FOR HOTELS AND RESTAURANTS

To give you an idea of hotel and restaurant prices, you'll find an indication next to the address. The hotel prices mentioned are - unless otherwise stated - per double room per night. The restaurant prices are - unless otherwise stated - an indication of the average price of a main course.

THE GERMAN WAY OF LIFE

The German (and especially the Berlin) way of life is a bit different than what people are accustomed to in the United States and other parts of Europe. Opening hours of shops and restaurants vary greatly, for one thing. Some are open only a few days a week, others not before 2pm. Generally, shops are open until 8pm on weekdays as well as on Saturdays. All shops are closed on Sundays. Most restaurants serve food all day, and at some you can eat until way past midnight.

Eating is not at the center of most Berliners' lives. Many eat on the streets in one of thousands of Wurst places or Döner Kebab huts. The art of cooking has only recently been introduced as a pastime by new arrivals from more southern parts of Germany. Perhaps this is because the sandy Berlin soil doesn't provide the same kinds of delicious fruits and vegetables as in other parts of the country. Nonetheless, food culture has grown in recent years, with the opening of many gourmet restaurants, pasta bars and Asian restaurants. Organic and health food stores can now be found all over the city, especially in the eastern boroughs of Mitte and Prenzlauer Berg, where they are practically on every corner.

Tipping is not obligatory in Berlin, but is always appreciated. Tips normally are about 10-15% of the bill.

One point to note about everyday communication: Berliners are famous for their unfriendliness. Don't be intimated however; simply return a rough comment with a rough answer. This seems to warm the hearts of most Berliners. It's a weird logic, but that's how people communicate in Berlin.

English is spoken almost everywhere in former West Berlin, where people learned English in school. In the East however, some people (especially those over thirty years old) have problems with basic English... they were raised with Russian!

PUBLIC HOLIDAYS

There are a few German holidays visitors should be aware of. On these days, shops are generally closed and museums and cultural sites have varying opening hours. In addition to religious holidays such as 'Karfreitag' (Good Friday), 'Ostermontag' (Easter Monday), 'Christi Himmelfahrt' (Ascension Day), 'Pfingsten' (Whitsun) and 'Weihnachten' (Christmas Eve, Christmas Day and Boxing Day), Germans observe the following public holidays:

1 January	- New Year's Day
1 May	- May (Labor) Day
3 October	- Celebration of East and West German unification

DO YOU HAVE ANY SUGGESTIONS FOR US?

We've tried to compile this guide with the utmost care. However, the selection of shops and restaurants can change quite frequently in Berlin. Should you no longer be able to find a certain address or have other comments or tips for us concerning this guide, please let us know. You'll find our address in the back of the book.

Hotels

In Berlin there is a huge variety of hotels in all price ranges, from well-known chains to private accommodation, allowing you to decide just how luxurious and expensive you'd like your accommodation to be. Below are a number of comfortable suggestions to fit every budget. You can find the letters on the overview map in the front of the book. The prices mentioned, unless otherwise specified, are per double room, per night, excluding breakfast.

Visit *www.berlin-hotels-germany.com*, *www.berlin-hotels-discount.com* or *www.berlin-info.de/english/hotels* for a further selection of hotels.

Low Range

(A) 'A little piece of Bavaria in the heart of Berlin' is the slogan of **Andechser Hof** in Mitte. Indeed, the rooms are full of Bavarian features and the ground floor restaurant serves delicious, homemade Bavarian and Austrian food. On quiet Ackerstrasse but still in the heart of Mitte, this basic hotel is the perfect place for budget travelers, offering a clean atmosphere and TV in every room.
ackerstrasse 154, mitte, telephone 030 28 09 78 44, www.andechserhof.de, price from €70, u-bahnhof rosenthaler platz

(B) **Hotel am Scheunenviertel** is located in the heart of the action, near the Museumsinsel, Hackesche Höfe and Friedrichsstrasse. An excellent value. The rooms are very clean, each with WC and shower. Breakfast is included, although there are some very good breakfast cafés just around the corner. Be sure to book in advance, as this hotel only has 18 rooms.
oranienburger strasse 38, mitte, telephone 030 282 21 25, www.hotelas.com, price from €80, s-bahnhof oranienburgerstrasse or u-bahnhof oranienburger tor

(c) Since **Artist Hotel Die Loge** is on one of the busiest streets in Mitte, it's a perfect choice for those who enjoy nightlife. It's only a few minutes to Mitte's bars and clubs, and the managers are familiar with demands for late checkouts. The beds are not the comfiest and WC and showers are shared, but the price is very modest.

friedrichstrasse 115, mitte, telephone 030 280 75 13, price from €60, u-bahnhof oranienburger tor

Mid Range

(D) **Alexander Plaza** is a nicely renovated hotel which houses a very modern establishment. Although it's just two minutes from Mitte's heart, the Hackesche Höfe, right where everything happens at night, it manages to be very quiet.

rosenstrasse 1, mitte, telephone 030 24 00 10, www.alexander-plaza.com, price from €155, s-bahnhof hackescher markt

(E) **Art Otel** is dedicated to the work of German painter Georg Baselitz, whose original work is displayed in all rooms and corridors. The ambience is very appealing - sort of Rococo meets Postmodernism.

wallstrasse 70-73, mitte, telephone 030 24 06 20, www.artotel.de, price from €128, u-bahnhof märkisches museum

(F) **The Park Inn** at Alexander Platz used to be the GDR's most spectacular hotel, residing in a skyscraper overlooking the whole of Berlin Mitte. Restored under American guidance, it still reeks of GDR authenticity and each room offers a fantastic view. This is a great place to stay in order to explore the adjoining Scheunenviertel and Eastern parts of Berlin, which can be easily reached from the nearby Alexanderplatz station. At the top of the hotel there's a casino, but don't expect to see people dressed up in Monaco style; men only have to wear a tie here.

alexanderplatz 1, mitte, telephone 030 238 90, www.parkinn.com, price from €102, u & s-bahnhof alexander platz

(G) **Hotel Unter den Linden**, built in GDR times and newly renovated, is located right next to Friedrichstrasse and Unter den Linden, Berlin's heartbeat. The rooms are not big, but they are clean and decorated with an interesting mix of styles (the tiling in the bathrooms is something you have to get used to). This is a great place to stay if you like to be based in a very central spot without paying the prices of other hotels in the same area.
unter den linden 14, mitte, telephone 030 23 81 10,
www.hotel-unter-den-linden.de, price from €98, s-bahnhof friedrichstrasse

(H) **Honigmond Garden Hotel** is one of the most romantic hotels in Mitte - "Honigmond" is the German word for honeymoon. In GDR times the hotel's yard was a nursery and now it's a green oasis of silence - a nice place to relax after walking around Berlin all day. Try to choose a room with a garden view, as in the evening hours you can hear birds singing and it feels like being in the countryside, even though the hotel is located right in the center of Berlin. All rooms have private bathrooms and are very reasonably priced.
invalidenstrasse 122, telephone 030 281 00 77, www.honigmond-berlin.de,
price from €65, s-bahnhof nordbahnhof or u-bahnhof zinnowitzer strasse

(I) **The Riverside Hotel** is a small and charming hotel that offers one of the most beautiful views in all of Mitte. Located alongside the Spree River, if you look out of one of the double bedrooms you can watch small boats sail past, and see the Reichstag and the Berliner Ensemble. Rooms with a view are available from €130-150, and are definitely worth it. The single bedrooms don't offer the same vista, but if you take a seat at the bar the view is equally nice.
friedrichstrasse 106, telephone 030 28 49 00, www.tolles-hotel.de,
price from €90, s-bahnhof friedrichstrasse

Ⓙ **SORAT ART'OTEL BERLIN**

High End

(J) **Sorat Art'otel Berlin**, a few seconds off Ku'damm, was decorated by German artist Wolf Vostell, and his collages and prints adorn the walls. The modern rooms are tastefully designed and have huge bathrooms. Ask for the "Eckzimmer" (corner rooms), which are the best and won't cost more. A breakfast buffet is included. This is the perfect hotel if you like the quieter and more luxurious West Berlin lifestyle.
joachimstaler strasse 29, charlottenburg, telephone 030 88 44 70,
www.sorat-hotels.com, price from €147, u-bahnhof berlin-zoologischer garten

(K) **The Hyatt Hotel** is just a minute from Potsdamer Platz and right opposite the Philarmonie, and Neue National Galerie - basically, right in the center of newly constructed Berlin. During the Berlinale film festival, the hotel is filled with film stars and at other times of the year it's a very popular choice for business people and tourists who enjoy the luxuries of the tastefully designed rooms and the excellent service. Although the hotel is located right in the city center, the rooms are quiet and there is a great spa to relax in.
marlene-dietrich-platz 2, tiergarten, telephone 030 25 53 12 34,
http://berlin.grand.hyatt.com, price from €240, s-bahnhof potsdamer platz

(L) One of the plushest and most spacious hotels in Berlin, **the Hotel Intercontinental** is perfect for people with a generous expense account. The rooms are extraordinarily large, tastefully decorated and have luxurious bathrooms. Even the lobby is a nice place to hang out; the soft leather chairs are a perfect place to read your guidebook and prepare to explore the city.
budapester strasse 2, tiergarten, telephone 030 260 20,
www.berlin.intercontinental.com, price from €235, u & s-bahnhof
zoologischer garten

Transportation

The public transportation system in Berlin is well planned. There is hardly a corner in the central parts of the city where you can't catch a public transport vehicle, be it a bus, Strassenbahn (street car), U-Bahn (subway) or S-Bahn (fast train). A ticket in central zones A and B cost €2,30, which allows you to travel for two hours on any mode of transportation. Other options include the 'Kurz-strecke' (short distance ticket), for three U-Bahn stops or two S-Bahn stops, and daily passes. Ticket machines offer services in most major world languages. For further information, call the Berlin traffic authority BVG at 030 19 449.

One of the most popular bus lines for tourists is the 100 **bus**, which offers a bargain sightseeing tour between Alexanderplatz and the Zoo station, passing the Brandenburg Gate and Unter den Linden, the Reichstag, Tiergarten, the Siegessäule and the Strasse des 17. Juni.

The **Strassenbahns**, **U-Bahns** and **S-Bahns** regularly run from 5.30 am to 00.45 am. On weekends, some U-Bahns and S-Bahns run all night. There is also a network of night buses that cross the city, marked with the letter 'N'.

You can hail **taxis** on the street or order them by phone. Würfelfunk, the biggest provider, is reachable at 030 210 10 10. Other essential taxi services can be reached at 030 690 22 or 030 44 33 22. Most taxis are Mercedes; if you want a station wagon, ask for a 'combi'. Taxi rates in Berlin are very moderate and there is no extra charge for luggage. If you just want to ride a short distance, hail a taxi on the street and ask for 'Kurzstrecke', or short trip, which will only cost €3 for a 2km trip.

In summertime, you'll see the rent-a-bike **bicycles** by the German rail (DB), which can easily be rented if you have a credit card. Just call the phone number on the side of the bike and a friendly person on the other end will ask you for your credit card details. As soon as you've registered, you'll receive a code with which you can open the bike's lock. The rates are reasonable (€1,50 for 30 minutes) and the best thing is that, because of the bike's GPS system, you can leave it anywhere you want. When you're finished, just redial the number and you'll receive the lock-up code; leave a message

ZENTRALFLUGHAFEN

TEMPELHOF

on an answering machine saying where you left the bike and just walk away. A central computer automatically registers where the bike has moved. It's a great idea and a very comfortable and easy way of getting around the city.

If you're too lazy to ride a bicycle of your own, you can also jump into a **Velo taxi**, a rickshaw-type vehicle that you can hail on the street or order on 030 44 35 89 90.

Berlin has three **airports**: Schönefeld, Tempelhof and Tegel. When leaving Berlin, always make sure to head for the right airport. If you take a cab, make sure to specifically name your airport. All the airports can be reached by public transport. There are express buses from both Zoo station and Alexanderplatz, which take 20 to 35 minutes; Tempelhof and Tegel can also be reached by U-Bahn within less than 30 minutes from all parts of town. Schönefeld, which is out of town, can be reached by S-Bahn, a trip that will take at least 40 minutes. A taxi ride will take the same amount of time, but will cost up to €50.

Mitte North

The northern part of Mitte is one of Berlin's most vibrant areas. At night this is where the action is, while during the day it's a great area to walk around. Most of all, the Scheunenviertel quarter is where the city's burgeoning cultural scene flourishes - a scene that has largely shaped the recent image of Berlin as the culture capital of Germany and one of Europe's youngest and trendiest cities.

Historically, this area was the center of Berlin's Jewish community, the beautiful synagogue on Oranienburger Strasse being the most

visible sign of its former glory. After the wall came down, squatters occupied the Scheunenviertel's empty houses. Rent was cheap or nonexistent and this was soon taken advantage of spawning the birth of new art galleries and other cultural centers. Today this is one of the few areas where business and culture thrive. Mostly, though, this is the area for entertainment, with tons of bars, restaurants, nightclubs, theaters and cinemas along Oranienburger Strasse and around the area of Hackesche Höfe. By the way: Mitte means middle, and this truly is the center of the city.

9 Musts!

Alte Schönhauser Strasse

Looking for Berlin fashion? You'll find it here.

Monsieur Vuong

Delicious Vietnamese food in a friendly environment

Hakesche Höfe

Enjoy the vibrant atmosphere of one of Berlin's busiest spots

Barcomi's

Grab fresh bagels, coffee and excellent cakes

Heckman Höfe

Deluxe second-hand shopping all in one square

Neue Synagogue

The former center of Jewish Berlin

Oranienbruger Strasse

This street is hot at night

Dada Falafel

Try the best falafel in town

Alexanderplatz

GDR architecture at its best

 Sights

Shopping

 Food & drink

 Nice to do

Sights

(11) **Hackesche Höfe** was formerly used as an old trading spot and is now very popular amongst tourists and Berliners alike. Full of bars, shops, cinemas, theaters and nightclubs, it's most vibrant at night.
hackescher markt, telephone 030 28 09 80 10, www.hackesche-hoefe.com, open daily 24 hours, admission free, s-bahnhof hackescher markt

(14) **Kunstwerke** is one of the best-known addresses for contemporary art in Berlin. A former butter factory, there's now an exhibition hall combined with studios. Many famous contemporary artists have been exhibited here and some work in the adjoining studios. The café in the yard is also worth visiting.
auguststrasse 69, telephone 030 243 45 90, www.kunstwerke-berlin.de, open fri-wed noon-20-6pm, thu noon-8pm, admission varies, s-bahnhof oranienburger strasse

(15) Beside the Hackesche Höfe, the **Heckmann Höfe** is one of the most popular yards in Mitte. With its small fountain in the middle, and its trees, bars and small shops, it resembles an Italian piazza. From here you get a good view of the back of the Neue Synagogue.
between auguststrasse 9 and oranienburger strasse 32, www.heckmann-hoefe.de, open 24 hours a day, s-bahnhof oranienburger tor

(17) Built in the mid-19th century, the **Neue Synagogue** was the showpiece of Berlin's Jewish community until it was attacked during Kristallnacht in 1939 and destroyed by allied bombs in 1945. Newly renovated, today it hosts an excellent exhibition on Jewish life in Berlin.
oranienburger strasse 28-30, telephone 030 88 02 84 51, www.cjudaicum.de, open sun-thu 10am-6pm, fri 10am-2pm, admission €5, s-bahnhof oranien-burger strasse

(20) The **Berliner Ensemble** is one of Berlin's smallest yet most beautiful and important theaters. Built in 1892, it hosted seminal directors such as Max Reinhardt and Bertolt Brecht, whose pieces are regularly featured here. Today, leading dramaturgists of the German theater show their work here.
bertolt-brecht-platz 1, telephone 030 28 40 81 55, www.berliner-ensemble.de, ticket box open mon-fri 8am-6pm, sat-sun 11am-6pm, admission varies, s-bahnhof friedrichstrasse

(23) Although almost completely destroyed in the Second World War, the **Museums Insel** is now almost fully renovated and hosts some of Berlin's finest historic museums, such as the Alte Museum, the Alte Nationalgalerie, the Bodemuseum (under construction till October 2005) and the Pergamon-museum. It's possible to spend a whole day here.
bodestrasse 1-3, telephone 030 20 90 55 66, www.smb.spk-berlin.de, most museums open tue-sun 10am-6pm, admission varies, s-bahnhof friedrichstrasse

(24) Erich Honecker, former president of the GDR, resided at **Staatsrats-gebäude** until 1989. The colorful windows inside still display GDR art illustrating the former socialist rule.
schlossplatz 1, open daily 9am-7.30pm, admission free, s-bahnhof alexanderplatz

(25) **Fernsehturm** am Alexanderplatz is both Berlin's and Germany's tallest building, standing at 207 meters. From the revolving restaurant at its top there is a fabulous view of the city.
panoramastrasse 1a, telephone 030 242 33 33, www.berlinerfernsehturm.de, open march-october daily 9am-1am, november-february 10am-midnight, admission € 8, u & s-bahnhof alexanderplatz

㉗ **Alexanderplatz** is one of the biggest squares in Berlin, and possibly one of the most historically relevant places in Berlin's history. In the 1920s this was the center of roaring Berlin, and Alfred Döblin's famous book on the Weimar times was named after it. In World War II, it was almost completely destroyed, except for the two Berolina houses that still remain today. In GDR years the square hosted parades and, in 1989, the biggest demonstration against the socialist GDR regime. Now it's a shopping area and central station for East Berlin's public transportation system.

alexanderplatz, u & s-bahnhof alexanderplatz

Food & Drink

(1) **Nola's**, in the small park at Weinbergsweg, is the perfect place to start off your walk through Mitte. In warm weather, enjoy a Mediterranean breakfast or a simple café au lait on the giant terrace, and in winter warm yourself with a nice cup of tea or soup on the sofas in the corner. Great for both breakfast and lunch, Nola's is one of Mitte's most popular spots.
veteranenstrasse 9, telephone 030 44 04 07 66, open sun-thu 10am-2am, fri-sat 10am-4am, price €6, u-bahnhof rosenthaler platz

(2) At night **Muj Facil** is always busy with the usual mix of media types, artists and actors who enjoy the meaty Brazilian dishes and loud Bossa Nova. During the day it's a rather quiet place for a pricey lunch. Muj Facil's terrace, open in summer, looks out on to a lovely old cemetery.
gormannstrasse 2, telephone 030 28 59 90 26, open daily 10am-2am, price €10, u-bahnhof weinmeisterstrasse

(4) Another great place for breakfast and lunch is the **Blaues Band** (blue ribbon). It's right at the top of Alte Schönhauser Strasse, Mitte's hippest shopping street, so it's a good place to get charged up for a shopping spree. Try the maple syrup pancakes, which are awesome.
alte schönhauser strasse 7-8, telephone 030 28 38 50 99, open 10am-2am, price €6, u-bahnhof weinmeisterstrasse

(7) Undoubtedly one of Mitte's most popular eateries, **Monsieur Vuong** is always packed. You might wait a few minutes to get seated, but when you do you'll join a mix of locals and tourists who all love Monsieur Vuong's light, tasty Vietnamese dishes. Don't forget to order the sweet Vietnamese espresso after dinner.
alte schönhauser strasse 46, telephone 030 30 87 26 43, open mon-sat noon-midnight, price €8, u-bahnhof weinmeisterstrasse

BLAUES BAND ④

(13) It's been around since the early days of the new Berlin Mitte, and **Barcomi's** is still one of the best places for a quality breakfast or a superb cake in the afternoon. An American who moved to Berlin more than a decade ago is in charge here, importing a variety of healthy delicacies from the States. Don't miss the New York cheesecake or the great lentil salad. Everything is available for take out as well.

sophienstrasse 21, telephone 030 28 59 83 63, open mon-sat 9am-10pm, price €7, s-bahnhof hackescher markt

(18) **Kamala** is a good place to recharge your batteries. The restaurant offers a huge variety of Thai and Vietnamese dishes that are not too heavy to digest, tasty and fresh - perfect for a quick break.

oranienburger strasse 69, telephone 030 283 27 97, open mon-thu 11.30am-midnight, fri-sat 11.30am-1am, price €9, s-bahnhof oranienburger strasse

(19) If you enjoy Middle Eastern delicacies, drop by **Dada Falafel**, which serves Berlin's freshest falafel and hummus. Also highly recommended is the orange/carrot juice, which goes very well with a plate of shawarma.

linienstrasse 132, telephone 030 282 83 17, open daily 11am-2am, price €4, u-bahnhof oranienburger tor

(21) Do your feet a favor and take a relaxed break at the **Tadschikische Teestube**, located in the upper floor of the former Hungarian embassy. Enter the stairs and turn left and you'll find yourself in the coziest tearoom, where you leave your shoes at the door and sit or lie on big cushions at low tables enjoying a fantastic range of teas. Expect original music and original tea combinations, such as the sparkling wine tea or the famous samovar, served with a piece of cake.

am festungsgraben 1, telephone 030 204 11 12, open mon-fri 5pm-midnight, sat-sun 3pm-midnight, price €4, s-bahnhof friedrichstrasse

Shopping

(3) The interior of **Holly's** is very elegant, your first sign that this is a tasteful shop. On the shelves are well tailored and highly individualistic, yet classic, designs by the shop's owners, Claudia Winkler and Christian Breil, as well as designs by up-and-coming Berlin fashion talent. Only limited editions of these clothes are for sale - one reason why this shop is increasingly popular with celebrities and 'fashionistas'.
alte schönhauser strasse 4, telephone 030 97 89 49 94, open tue-fri noon-8pm, sat noon-5 pm, u-bahnhof rosa luxemburg platz

(5) When an art historian, an architect and an artist opened **Pro Qm** at the height of the New Economy boom in 1999, people called them nuts. Why start a bookstore when practically anyone can order books through Amazon.com? A few years later, the store has successfully proved itself to be Mitte's hippest bookstore, stocking books from art to cultural studies, architecture and fashion. Tons of international art and fashion magazines are available as well.
alte schönhauser strasse 48, telephone 030 24 72 85 20, open mon-fri noon-8pm, sat 11am-4pm, u- bahnhof rosa luxemburg platz

(6) Danish design is what you'll find at **Stue** (Danish for living room). Whether it's furniture, lamps, ceramics or glass, Marie Rädiker refreshes her selection every month by traveling to Denmark to handpick the merchandise. If you've got the time, try to visit this shop more than once.
alte schönhauser strasse 48, telephone 030 24 72 76 50, open mon-fri 2pm-7pm, sat 1pm-5pm, u-bahnhof weinmeisterstrasse

(8) If you are into fancy plastic bags, funky flip-flops or Jesus statues, **O.K. Versand** is the shop for you. The shop is very popular amongst Berlin's interior design fans, especially those that love to shop for stuff that has a funny and trashy edge and is super-inexpensive. You're sure to find unique gifts here.
alte schönhauser strasse 36-37, telephone 030 24 63 87 46, open mon-fri noon-8pm, sat noon-4pm, u-bahnhof weinmeisterstrasse

(9) The giant-sized jet bed in the center of this shop says it all. This is where women find the things that make them look good horizontal. Babydolls, plush high heels… at **Blush** you'll find seductive underwear and lingerie that looks sexy but doesn't look cheap. Brands such as Paul Smith Woman are available as well as designs by shop owner Claudia Kleinert.

alte schönhauser strasse 25, telephone 030 42 02 27 01, open mon-thu 10.30am-7.30pm, fri 10.30am-8pm, sat 10.30am-5pm, u-bahnhof wein-meisterstrasse

(10) A mix of design gallery and shop, **Authentics** stocks all sorts of living accessories by international design talent. Have a look at their online shop to see what's in stock: www.authentics.de.

alte schönhauser strasse 19, telephone 030 28 09 92 92, open mon-fri noon-8pm, sat 11am-4pm, u-bahnhof weinmeisterstrasse

(12) In Japan, the wooden-soled **Trippen** shoes are very sought after; at the Hackesche Höfe, this Berlin brand has its flagship store. You'll find every-thing from sandals to boots here; by the way, clogs have never been more fashionable!

hackesche höfe, rosenthalerstrasse 40-41, telephone 030 28 39 13 37, open mon-fri noon-7pm, sat 10am-5pm, s-bahnhof hackescher markt

(16) At **Sterling Gold**, you'll find the most elegant secondhand eveningwear from more than sixty years of fashion. Hundreds of super luxurious gowns hang in the shop, and you can try them all on. If one doesn't fit right, a tailor will give a helping hand.

heckmannhöfe, oranienburgerstrasse 32, telephone 030 28 09 65 00, open mon-fri noon-8pm, sat noon-4pm, s-bahnhof oranienburger strasse

Nice to do

(22) If you walk the museum island on weekends, you'll pass a small **flea market** on the banks of the Spree channel which runs alongside the island. Here you'll find pottery and books and GDR and CCCP nostalgia. A great place to pick up real Berlin souvenirs...
around the museum island, bodestrasse, open sat-sun 10am-4pm, s-bahnhof friedrichstrasse

(26) Want to know what time it is? Well, the **Weltzeituhr** (global time clock) displays the global time in true fashion. You have to figure it out however, as this huge clock was built in pre digital times, (i.e. 1969). It's a stylish reminder of GDR modernism and one of the prime icons of East Berlin. A great place to have a photo taken.
alexanderplatz, s-bahnhof alexanderplatz

Mitte North

Start your walk around lunchtime, because many shops in Mitte won't open before noon. Go from Weinbergswegpark (1) south via Rosenthaler Platz, then left on Linienstrasse. While walking, have a look at original GDR architecture for communal housing. Take the first street, Gormannstrasse, to the right (2), proceed and then turn left into Mulackstrasse until you reach Alte Schönhauser Strasse. Mulackstrasse was, in the 1920s, the street where the first tolerated gay bars were located. Turn left (3) (4) and back again down the Alte Schönhauserstrasse (5) (6) (7) (8) (9) (10) for serious shopping or another snack. Cross Weinmeisterstrasse and continue till you reach Rosenthaler Strasse. Turn left to Hackesche Höfe (11) (12), walk through the Höfe to Sophienstrasse (13), through the Sophie-Gips-Höfe until you're on Gipsstrasse, and then turn left up the street to Auguststrasse (14). Shortly before you reach Tucholskystrasse, search for the entrance to the Heckmann Höfe (15) (16) through which you can walk to Oranienburger Strasse to the left (17) or the right (18) (19). Follow Oranienburger Strasse to the right until you reach Friedrichstrasse. To the left you'll see the Tacheles, which used to be a warehouse and is now a center for young art. At Friedrichstrasse, turn left and walk towards the Spree bridge, then turn right for Bertolt Brecht platz (20). Return to Friedrichstrasse and head towards the Friedrichstrasse station; continue and then turn left on Dorotheenstrasse. Take the second street, Universitätsstrasse, to the right until you reach Unter den Linden. Turn left, pass the Humboldt University, and the historic museum. On the opposite side is the Bebelplatz, which became famous when Nazis burned books there in 1933. After the museum and over the bridge, turn left, walk through the Lustgarten alongside the Spree for teatime (21). Turn right to Bodestrasse (22) (23). Walk towards Karl-Liebknecht-Strasse via the dome, cross the street (24) and walk to the left towards the TV tower (25). If you like, take the elevator up the tower for a coffee or just proceed to the Weltzeituhr (26) for some snapshots. Alexanderplatz (27) is great for public transport. Just jump into the U- or S-Bahn at Alexanderplatz station.

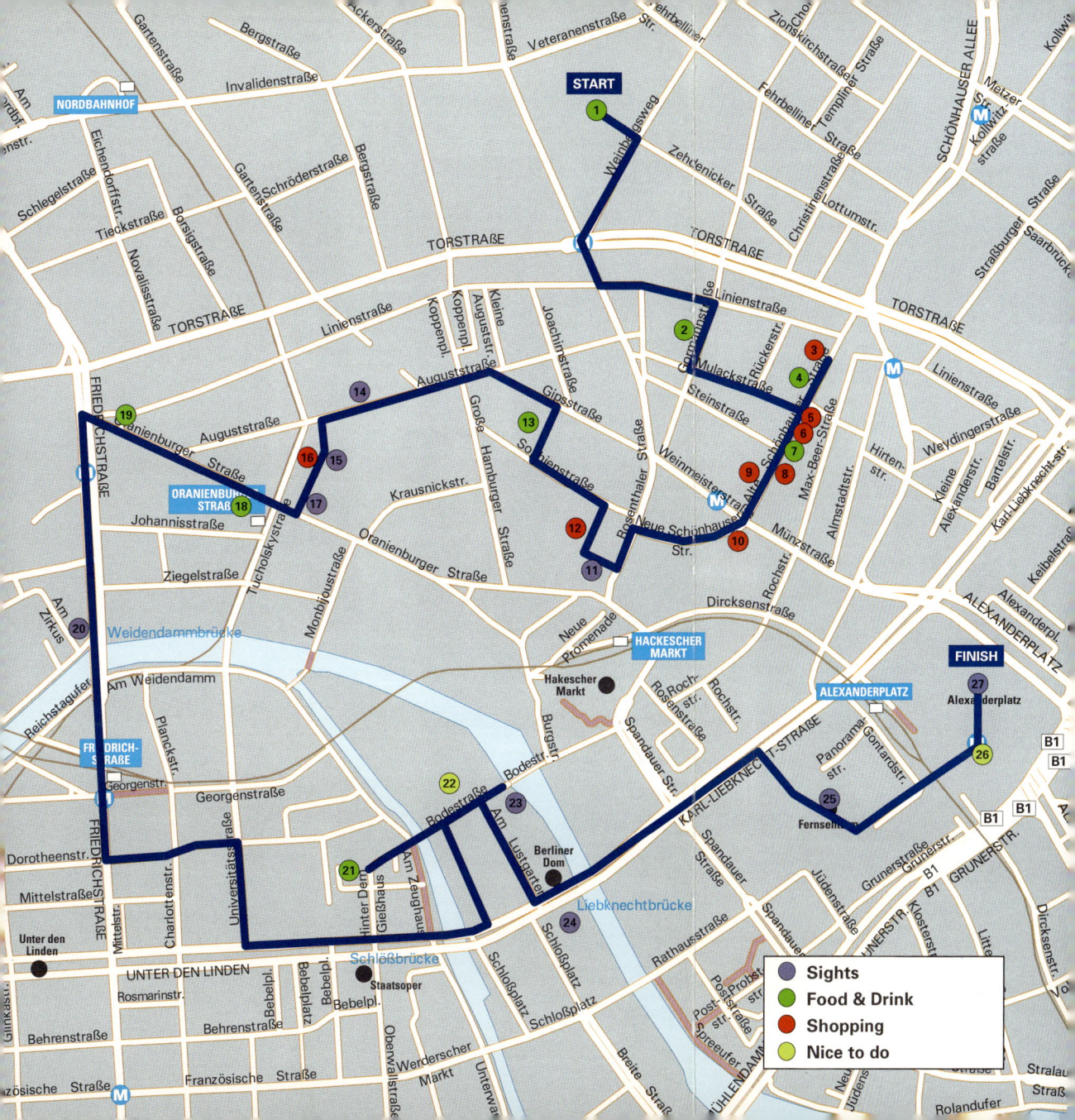

Prenzlauer Berg

Along with Mitte, Prenzlauer Berg is the most popular part of former East Berlin. Largely a residential area, it is full of little shops, restaurants and bars. To the south, Prenzlauer Berg is young and very hip, with streets like Kastanienallee, which almost has a catwalk-like feel to it - locals call it the 'Castingallee'. The Kollwitzplatz area used to be an artist's neighborhood and is now very chic and home to many young families and entrepreneurs. At night, this is where Prenzlbergers (as residents call themselves) go for dinner and drinks. Unfortunately it has also become a tourist trap, but if you stroll the side streets you can separate yourself from the busloads.

- 🟣 **Sights**
- 🟢 **Food & Drink**
- 🔴 **Shopping**
- 🟡 **Nice to do**

2

To the north lies Helmholtzplatz, which tourists haven't yet discovered. The crowd here is more local and slightly younger than on Kollwitzplatz. Here you'll find many nice restaurants and bars. In the western part of Prenzlauer Berg are Mauerpark and Bernauerstrasse, which used to be one of the main streets where the wall separated East and West Berlin. Look for the brick stripes on the pavement to see where the wall used to be. For an extensive look at the city's recent history, especially the 'wall years', visit the documentation center on Bernauerstrasse.

9 Musts!

Kulturbrauerei

Check out the
restaurants, pubs
and cinemas

Kollwitzplatz

Promenade on
Prenzlauers Berg's
prettiest square

Gugelhof

Sit at the table where
Bill Clinton dined

Knaackstrasse

Visit antique shops,
boutiques and
cozy restaurants

Delizie D'Italia

Taste delicious
homemade pasta
at bargain prices

Weinstein

Enjoy super wines,
excellent dishes and
a quaint atmosphere

Konopke

Don't miss
the city's best original
Berlin Currywurst

Mauerpark

Meet young
Prenzlbergers

Documentation center

See original remains
of the wall

 Sights

 Food & drink

Shopping

 Nice to do

Sights

(4) In its early incarnation, the **Kulturbrauerei** used to be a brewery where one of the dozens of Berlin beers was brewed. Now the freshly renovated buildings are home to a cinema and some bars, and there are lectures and hot salsa parties at Soda club.
knaackstrasse 97, telephone 030 44 31 50, www.kulturbrauerei.de, open daily 10am-open end, u-bahnhof eberswalder strasse

(7) Shortly after the wall fell, the picturesque **Kollwitzplatz** rose to prominence because of its beautiful old houses. First it was artists and intellectuals, now it's tourists that roam the streets. Nevertheless, the square hasn't lost its attractiveness. There are lots of restaurants, bars, and small shops with unique fashion, health food and Italian delicacy stores.
kollwitzplatz, u-bahnhof senefelderplatz

(23) **Mauerpark** is a very popular spot to relax and play in the densely populated Prenzlauer Berg. Sometimes overcrowded with squatter types and their dogs, in summer it's a meeting point for all kinds of Prenzlbergers.
schwedter strasse, corner bernauer strasse, open daily 24 hours, u-bahnhof eberswalder strasse

(24) The **Berlin Wall Documentation Center** is part of the memorial complex on Bernauerstrasse that consists of the chapel of fraternization, the memorial site and the documentation center. In the center, historical information about the wall and its political, cultural and social effects is displayed. Opposite the center, there are original pieces of the wall left. It's a frightening yet impressive display of the effects of a political system.
bernauer strasse 111, telephone 030 464 10 30, open wed-sun 10am-5pm, www.berliner-mauer-dokumentationszentrum.de, no admission, s-bahnhof nordbahnhof

bon
appétit

Food & Drink

(1) **Makom** has been a pub and café since 1918 and you can still spot some of the original wall paintings from the early days. Russian and Polish is the focus of the menu at Makom, while tango and chansons from the 20s pour from the stereo. This is a beautiful place, and not only for the nostalgic.
zionskirchplatz 39, telephone 030 449 01 29, open daily 10am-3am, price €5, u-bahnhof brunnenstrasse

(6) **Gugelhof** serves specialties from Alsace, the region between southwest Germany and eastern France well known for its cakes and meat dishes. Former U.S. President Bill Clinton dined here in the mid 1990s, when visiting Berlin and ever since it has become a tourist attraction. The food has remained high quality in spite of the tourist influx.
knaackstrasse 37, telephone 030 442 92 29, open daily 10am-1am, price €13, u-bahnhof senefelder platz

(8) Of all cafés and bars at Wasserturmplatz, the **Anita Wronski** is the place where the sun shines the longest in the afternoon. Little wonder, then, that the café is second home to dozens of neighborhood students and workers who spend their days reading, chatting or just hanging out. If you want to meet Berliners, this is the place to do it.
knaackstrasse 26-28, telephone 030 442 84 83, open mon-fri 9am-2am, sat-sun 10am-2am, price € 4, u-bahnhof senefelder platz

(9) **Pasternak** is considered the leading restaurant for original Russian cooking in Berlin. Though the variety of regional specialties ranges from the Baltic Sea to the Himalayas, it's the Russian classics that are most highly recommended: Try the Borscht soup served with beans or the very tasty Soljanka. The meat dishes are good too, and the selection of vodka is outstanding. On Tuesdays and Thursdays live music plays.
knaackstrasse 22-24, telephone 030 441 33 99, open daily summer noon-1am, winter 6pm-1am, price €9, u-bahnhof senefelderplatz

⑭ When you see duck soup on the menu at **Mao Thai**, you can take it as a good sign that this is not your average Thai restaurant. Authenticity in food and ambience is what makes Mao Thai unique and it is indeed one of the best Thai restaurants in Berlin. Prices are a little high, but the fresh and delicate food gives so much joy, you won't regret the extra cost.

wörther strasse 30, telephone 030 441 92 61, open sun-thu noon-midnight, fri-sat noon-1am, price € 10, u-bahnhof senefelder platz

⑯ **Sowohlalsauch** is an Austrian coffee house offering the best cakes in Prenzlauer Berg. Try the amazing apple cake or the chocolate tart, and wash them down with one of the dozens of coffees on the menu. If you're not in the mood for cake, try the Viennese schnitzel.

kollwitzstrasse 88, telephone 030 332 93 11, open daily 9am-2am, price €6, u-bahnhof senefelder platz

⑰ **Delizie D'Italia** is probably the best 'enoteca' in Prenzlauer Berg. There are many Italian restaurants, but nowhere does the pasta taste so fresh and cost so little. At lunchtime, for example, you can have a giant plate of pasta for just €6. In addition to the excellent food, there are many Italian delicacies to take with you.

kollwitzstrasse 100, telephone 030 48 49 49 77, open mon-sat 11am-midnight, price €7, u-bahnhof senefelder platz

⑲ **Weinstein** is a cozy restaurant close to Helmholtzplatz, serving fabulous German, Alpine and French dishes alongside a list of super wines. Choose a dish and the waiter will suggest a selection of wines from Germany, Austria and France that will tickle your taste buds. A dinner at Weinstein is something you will remember for a long time.

lychener strasse 33, telephone 030 441 18 42, open mon-sat 5pm-2am, sun 6pm-2am, price €12, u-bahnhof eberswalder strasse

㉔ **Konopke** is world famous for its homemade 'currywurst' - a thick sausage topped with curry sauce considered a typical Berlin delicacy. From construction workers to businessmen, all Berliners eat at Konopke.
schönhauser allee 44a, telephone 030 442 77 65, open mon-fri 6am-8pm, price €1.50, u-bahnhof eberswalder strasse

㉑ The **Prater** is one of the oldest restaurants in Prenzlauer Berg and is one of the most original beer halls, serving solid German food. Today it's part of the Volksbühne complex, one of the most avant-garde theaters in town, keeping Prater's clientele young, academic and often accompanied by kids. The beautiful beer garden is a great place to spend a warm summer night.
kastanienallee 7-9, telephone 030 448 56 88, open mon-fri 6pm-1am, sat-sun 2pm-1am, price €7, u-bahnhof eberswalder strasse

㉕ **Locanda Pane** is a small, family run Italian restaurant with a daily menu. Guests come because of the handmade pasta, the impressive range of primi piatti and the fish and meat dishes. It's popular amongst people in the film business and, if you are lucky, you can rub shoulders with Wim Wenders, who stays nearby when he's in town.
ackerstrasse 16-17, telephone 030 28 38 77 22, open mon-fri noon-4pm, 6.30pm-midnight, sat 6.30pm-midnight, price €8, u-bahnhof rosenthaler platz

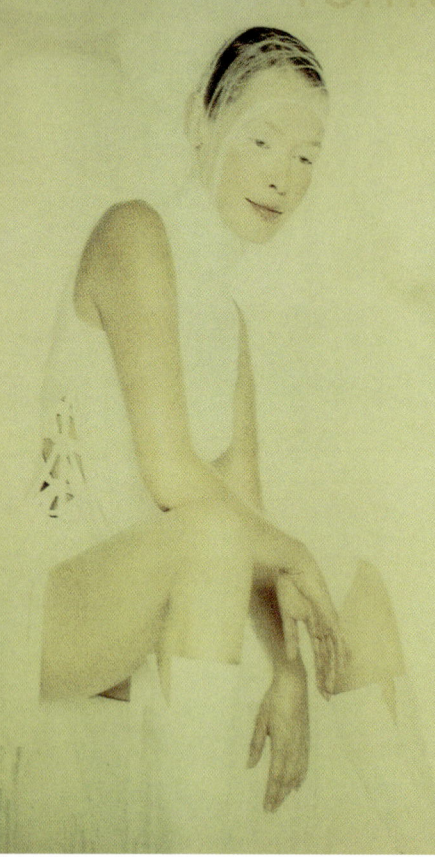

thatchers
remedy 2003

Shopping

(3) The name may be confusing, but it's surely one that people won't forget. **Thatcher's** is a fashion boutique run by two young Berlin designers who concoct extravagant and eye-catching clothes. Whether for parties, clubs or simple gatherings, this store is for those who want a special, unique wardrobe. Since the clothes are exclusive to this boutique, uniqueness is guaranteed.

kastanienallee 21, telephone 030 24 62 77 51, open mon-sat noon-7pm, u-bahnhof eberswalder strasse

(5) **Falbala** is not your average vintage clothing store. You won't find any early 1970's Prada bags or old-school YSL here, but you will find real vintage clothing up to 70 years old. No wonder people like designer Donna Karan come here to get inspired.

knaackstrasse 43, telephone 030 44 05 10 82, open mon-fri 1pm-6pm, sat noon-2pm, u-bahnhof senefelder platz

(10) Some of the women's clothes sold at **Schelpmeier** are designed by the shop's owner, but the majority of the clothes come from young, independent designers from Scandinavia, Holland and Germany. Chic and practical, everything has a classic cut and is made from colorful, natural fabrics.

rykestrasse 1, telephone 030 392 67 81, open mon-fr 11am-7pm, sat 11am-4pm, u-bahnhof senefelder platz

(11) There are many interior design shops around the Kollwitzplatz and Wasserturmplatz area, but at **Exedra** you'll find quality stuff at moderate prices. You'll especially find things for garden and terrace use, from lamps and wooden furniture to metal, steel work and pottery. If you're looking for a nice gift for your loved ones at home, you'll likely find it at Exedra. *rykestrasse 49, telephone 030 44 01 72 41, open mon-fri 11am-7pm, sat 11am-2pm, u-bahnhof senefelder platz*

(13) From the outside, **Georg Büchner Buchladen** looks like an average bookshop but inside is a vast range of German and international novels and academic books. Contrary to the paltry advice you might get in the mega-stores downtown, the employees at Georg Büchner seem to know everything about the books they carry and can give very elaborate explanations about the titles as well as recommendations for other authors and publications. *wörther strasse 10, telephone 030 378 33 42, open mon-fri 10am-7pm, sat 11am-2pm, u-bahnhof senefelder platz*

(22) If you are looking for a sporty Berlin souvenir, you'll find it at **Eisdieler**. Popular with students and music fans, this homegrown street wear brand produces everything from bags to shirts to shorts. Besides their own Eisdieler clothing, the shop also carries a selection of skate and surf brands. On trendy Kastanienallee, the Eisdieler brand is a common sight. *kastanienallee 12, telephone 030 285 73 51, open mon-fri noon-8pm, sat noon-6pm, u-bahnhof eberswalderstrasse*

BUCH
KUNST
PAPIER

GEORG-BÜCHNER
BUCHLADEN

Nice to do

② If you want to see where young, chic Berliners hang out, don't miss **Kastanienallee**. Called 'Castingallee' by locals, this is currently the hottest place to be. Students hang out here during the day and art, film, music and fashion mavens meet here at night to discuss future projects or gossip in the many cafés, bars and snack shops. Discover it before the tourists do.

kastanienallee, u-bahnhof rosenthaler platz or u-bahnhof eberswalder strasse.

⑫ The long, cold Berlin winter lasts from October to April and it's at the city's saunas where Berliners catch some warmth in the dark months. One favorite is the pleasant sauna at **Dampfbad Rykestrasse**. It's small and often busy, but a very nice place to relax and work up a sweat. There is a small stone garden and a cold bath, and if you'd like a massage you just have to ask. Remember that in Germany, people go nude to the sauna - a towel is the only cloth that is tolerated. Don't worry though... life is much easier in the nude.

rykestrasse 10, telephone 030 44 04 63 97, open daily noon-midnight, tue women only, u-bahnhof senefelder platz

⑮ The Saturday **organic food market** is very popular with the area's residents. You'll see an abundance of meat, vegetables, cheeses and pottery and also many small stands where alternative farmers from outside Berlin sell vegan sausages or hand-knitted socks. You'll smell and taste the difference right away. All the food sold here comes from organic farms - that is, the food is grown, raised and harvested in an eco-friendly manner.

kollwitzplatz, kollwitzstrasse, sat 8am-2pm, u-bahnhof senefelder platz

⑱ The **Zeiss Planetarium** was opened in 1987 as one of Europe's most modern star theaters. The entrance to the building opens to a spacious foyer with changing exhibits and a small café. In the auditorium upstairs, science is communicated in an effective way, blending education at and entertainment, facts and imagination into a multimedia experience in which an artificial sky as well as numerous astronomical phenomena are shown. It's a visual delight and a great alternative to going to the cinema.

prenzlauer allee 80, telephone 030 42 18 45 12, www.astw.de, open mon-tue, thu 9am-noon, wed 9am-12.30pm, 1.30pm-9pm, fri 9am-noon, 7.30pm-9pm, sat 1.30pm-9pm, sun 1.30pm-5pm, admission €5, s-bahnhof prenzlauer allee

Prenzlauer Berg

Begin your tour at lunchtime or for a late breakfast. As in Mitte, shops here open late. Start with a coffee at Makom ①, then walk up Kastanienallee ② ③. When you reach Oderbergerstrasse turn right, cross Schönhauser Allee on to Sredzkistrasse, turn left to the Knaackstrasse ④. Walk back to the Sredzkistrasse and turn left, continue straight ahead and when you've reached Husemannstrasse, turn right onto Kollwitzplatz ⑦. Turn right and enter Knaackstrasse to the left ⑤ ⑥; cross Kollwitzstrasse until you've reached the Wasserturmplatz, which is dominated by a huge, cylindrical building - a former water tank. Have a coffee at Anita Wronski ⑧ or some soup at Pasternak ⑨, then continue onto Rykestrasse ⑩ ⑪ ⑫, turn left ⑬ ⑭ back to Kollwitzplatz ⑮. Move up north on Kollwitzstrasse, and if you're ready for a piece of cake, go to Café Sowohlalsauch ⑯ or for a pasta break, check out Delizie D'Italia ⑰. Cross Danziger Strasse and head to Senefelder Strasse, then continue until you reach Hiddenseerstrasse. Turn right and continue to Prenzlauer Allee. On the other side you'll see the silver roof of the bubble-shaped planetarium ⑱. Cross Prenzlauer Allee to Staargaader Strasse, turn left on Dunckerstrasse, and continue to the square at Helmholtz-platz. Enter Lettestrasse, turn left at its end to Lychenerstrasse ⑲, at the next corner turn right on Raumerstrasse until you hit Pappelallee. Turn left towards U-Bahnhof Eberswalderstrasse. Continue and return to Kastanien-allee, after having a wurst at Konopke ⑳ or a beer at Prater ㉑. Proceed on Kastanienallee ㉒, turn to the right at Oderbergerstrasse at the end of which is Mauerpark ㉓. Walk down Bernauerstrasse, which used to be the street where the wall ran, splitting Prenzlauer Berg (the former East) from Wedding (the former West). The green strip to your left used to be the 'death strip'. After a kilometer you'll hit original parts of the Wall as well as the documentation center ㉔. After visiting the center, turn to Ackerstrasse, pass the huge Ackerstrasse cemetery until you've reached Invalidenstrasse, cross it and then to your left for Locanda Pane ㉕.

Mitte South

2

5

The southern part of Mitte is the area that represents the city's newfound power. The Reichstag, the Brandenburg gate and the restored area south of Unter den Linden and alongside Friedrichstrasse, with its exclusive shops, expensive hotels and embassy buildings, illustrate the regained significance of the city. Adjoining the area of the Reichstag is the biggest park in Berlin, the Tiergarten. Fans of the famous Wim Wenders movie 'Wings of Desire' will recognize the Siegessäule inside the park.

- 🟣 Sights
- 🟢 Food & Drink
- 🔴 Shopping
- ⚪ Nice to do

3

From the Siegessäule it's a short walk to Potsdamer Platz, the official cultural center of Berlin, with the Neue Nationalgalerie, the Stadtbibliothek as well as the philharmonic. Potsdamer Platz was the heart of 1930s Berlin, but was completely destroyed during World War II and was a vast, empty space during the cold war. Since the fall of the Berlin wall, it became Europe's biggest construction site, when the city started its large-scale reconstruction. Now almost finished, the Potsdamer Platz houses the headquarters of multinational corporations, cinemas, theaters, hotels, some restaurants and Potsdamer Platz Arkaden, a huge shopping mall. The area might not be beautiful, but it's worth a visit nevertheless.

9 Musts!

Café Einstein

Rub shoulders with politicians, enjoy the cakes

Brandenburg Gate

Walk through the symbol of Berlin

Reichstag

Get on top of the German parliament

Siegessäule

Climb up the tower for a great view

Neue Nationalgalerie

Gaze at Mies van der Rohe's modernist masterpiece

Potsdamer Platz

Walk through new Berlin

Checkpoint Charlie

See the original East-West border control post

Sale e Tabacchi

Eat where Berlin intellectuals gather

Friedrichstrasse

Shop till you drop in one of the warehouses

 **Sights**
 Food & drink
Shopping
Nice to do

② **BRANDENBURG GATE**

Sights

② The **Brandenburg Gate** is Berlin's, as well as Germany's, symbol. It's so symbolically important that it is pictured on one side of several German Euro coins, even though it never played an important functional role. Built in the late 18th century, the gate has seen many historic moments, from workers protests in the 1910s to Nazi marches in the 1930s. During the Cold War, the gate was stuck between two sides of the wall. Now it has become a must-see for tourists and a popular spot for mega-events of all kinds, when the Pariser Platz and other adjoining streets often get blocked off.
pariser platz, s-bahnhof unter den linden

③ The **Reichstag** has seen many changes in German history, from the proclamation of the Weimar republic from one of its windows to its burning in 1933 to Christo packing it up in the mid-90s and finally to the first governmental meeting in 1996. It is now home to the German government. When British architect Sir Norman Foster restructured the building and added a dome to it, the Reichstag became a tourist magnet and is a great place to not only trace Berlin and German history but also to enjoy a fantastic view from the roof terrace.
platz der republik 1, telephone 030 22 73 21 52, www.bundestag.de, open daily 8am-10pm, admission varies, s-bahnhof unter den linden

⑦ Built in 1968 as the West Berlin equivalent to the Museumsinsel, the **Kulturforum** was built on the vast gap that former Lützowplatz and Potsdamer Platz left behind. The slick Neue Nationalgalerie became its central symbol. Built by the former Berliner Bauhaus architect Mies van der Rohe, it is a masterpiece of modernism and remains a fascinating building and home to many changing exhibitions. At night, a permanent art installation by American artist Jenny Holzer turns the building into a futuristic glowing lamp.
potsdamer strasse 50, telephone 030 266 26 51, open tue, wed, fri 10am-6pm, thu 10am-10pm, sat-sun 11am-6pm, admission varies, u & s-bahnhof potsdamer platz

(8) In the 1920s, the **Potsdamer Platz** was Berlin's most congested square and a sign of the city's modernity. During Cold War times, the completely destroyed area was a vast and empty zone between the Berlin wall. Reconstruction started in 1993 for a new center of the German capital. In the following years the Potsdamer Platz caused a sensation as Europe's biggest construction site. Now almost completed, the square has become an important center for business and culture in the heart of Berlin.
potsdamer platz, u & s-bahnhof potsdamer platz

(10) On August 13th, 1961, armed GDR soldiers sealed off the city of West Berlin and construction of the Berlin Wall began. The house at **Checkpoint Charlie** is now a museum displaying the history of the Wall, including original objects of successful attempts to cross over, under and above the ground. Around the museum and the original remains of the checkpoint, which been featured in too many movies to mention, there are various stands selling memorabilia of all sorts, from Russian army hats to pieces of the Wall.
friedrichstrasse 44, telephone 030 253 72 50, www.checkpoint-charlie.de, open daily 9am-10pm, admission €7,50 adults, €4,50 children & students, u-bahnhof kochstrasse

(19) The **Gendarmenmarkt** is undoubtedly one of Berlin's prettiest squares, with its 19th century architecture and its two dome churches, the French dome and the German dome. Alongside the square there are many posh restaurants and cafés. In summer, there are open-air classical music concerts in front of the beautifully restored Konzerthaus. Many state receptions take place here, as well as film premiere parties. The area has consequently become a symbol for glitz and the city's newborn political and cultural power.
gendarmenmarkt, u-bahnhof stadtmitte

Food & Drink

(1) **Café Einstein** is situated on busy boulevard Unter den Linden and is a great place to start the day. In summer, you can sit outside in the sun watching passers-by, sipping an original Viennese melange and nibbling one of the superb cakes. If you like a quieter setting, have a seat inside, where politicians from the nearby Reichstag often enjoy lunch. Don't worry about the police standing next to the café… that is because of its location close to the American embassy.

unter den linden 42, telephone 030 204 36 32, open daily 7am-1am, price € 7, u-bahnhof friedrichstrasse

(4) The **Café im Haus der Kulturen der Welt** is recommended not so much for its coffee and cakes but because of its location behind the beautiful Haus der Kulturen der Welt with a view on the Spree river that shouldn't be missed. If you are into boat tours, this café is a good place to stop and catch one of the passing boats that will take you back to Mitte or further west on the Spree.

john-foster-dulles-allee 10, telephone 030 39 78 71 75, open tue-sun 10am-8pm, price €4, s-bahnhof lehrter stadtbahnhof

(11) **Sale e Tabacchi** is one of the most popular Italian restaurants in Berlin. Employees from the 'Tageszeitung', the leftist-alternative Berlin daily that resides in the same building, often have lunch here. At night, it's a popular spot amongst artists, journalists and intellectuals. A look at the menu reflects the high expectations of the restaurant's clientele. Reservations are recommended.

kochstrasse 18, telephone 030 25 29 50 03, open daily 9am-2am, price € 18, u-bahnhof kochstrasse

SALE E TABACCHI

RIV. N°38   RIV. N°38

(16) **Borchardts** is currently the trendiest Berlin restaurant. Seats are hard to get but if you're lucky (or charming) enough to snag a table, you can expect to enjoy fantastic service, a very good menu, excellent wines and a view of the city's elite. Businessmen from the adjoining area meet here for lunch, while at night you can sometimes see German chancellor Gerhard Schröder or Hollywood actor George Clooney having dinner. Being part of the scene is not a bargain though, evening menus start at €40 and the wines come with hefty price tags too.

französische strasse 47, telephone 030 20 38 71 10, open daily 11.30am-1am, price €30, u-bahnhof französische strasse

(17) **Seasons** is located in the Four Seasons hotel, and with its young American chef Drew Deckman, the restaurant is considered to be one among the city's most promising. Its cutting edge cooking combines French haute cuisine with freestyle elements from around the world. The food is so good and the service so immaculate that you'll quickly forget the ultra-conservative ambiance. The three-course business lunch for €29 is highly recommended.

charlottenstrasse 49, telephone 030 20 33 63 63, open daily noon-2pm, 6.30pm-11pm, price €30, u-bahnhof französische strasse

(18) **Lutter & Wegener** is close to Gendarmenmarkt, the heart of new business Berlin, so expect lots of suits & ties at this traditional restaurant, which has been around since the mid-19th century. German romanticist poets such as Heinrich Heine have dined here and ever since then, the excellent light German and Austrian cooking hasn't changed much. Besides the classic German meat dishes, a daily changing menu of light Mediterranean food is available. Ask for the wine list, which offers more than 1000 options.

charlottenstrasse 56, telephone 030 202 95 40, open daily 11am-3am, price €18, u-bahnhof französische strasse

⑳ Mutter Hoppe is close to the city's council, the Rote Rathaus, named after the color of its bricks, not its political agenda. For lunch, many local politicians enjoy the wholesome German and Berlin specialties on the menu. Highly recommended is the Schweinskrustenbraten (roasted pork with a crust) or an entire Spanferkel (suckling pig) for 8 people (and of course, the beer). This is definitely not a restaurant for vegetarians or fans of light cooking. Reservations are recommended for Fridays and Saturdays. *rathausstrasse 21, telephone 030 241 56 25, open daily 11.30am-1am, price €12, u-bahnhof alexanderplatz*

Shopping

⑫ Before World War II, **Friedrichstrasse** was Berlin's most popular street. Since the wall fell, much money has been poured in to revamp the street, which became run down in anti-consumerist GDR times. Friedrichstrasse has now reemerged as one of Berlin's busiest shopping streets, with a mix of chain stores and exclusive shopping malls such as Galeries Lafayette and the Quartier 206. When the street was reconstructed, architects unfortunately forgot to leave room for some green so it lacks a little atmosphere. Still, for serious shoppers this is a street worth seeing.

friedrichstrasse, u-bahnhof stadtmitte or französische strasse, s-bahnhof friedrichstrasse

⑬ **Leysieffer** is a Berlin-based pastry chain with branches all over the city. Known for its excellent cakes and tarts, you can also buy superb marmalades and chocolates here. Don't forget to grab some 'Rote Grütze' (red fruit jelly), a Berlin sweet specialty that matches perfectly with ice cream or yogurt.

friedrichstrasse 67, telephone 030 20 45 81 58, open mon-fri 10am-7pm, sat 10am-4pm, u-bahnhof stadtmitte

⑭ **Quartier 206** is a metropolitan department store spanning a number of floors. Satisfy your luxurious needs and wants with fashions from Prada to Donna Karan to Helmut Lang. If you need a break from shopping, have a seat at the Quartier café and watch the passers-by.

friedrichstrasse 71, telephone 030 20 94 60 00, open mon-fri 10am-8pm, sat 10am-4pm, u-bahnhof französische strasse

(15) The **Galeries Lafayette** on Friedrichstrasse is a branch of the famous Parisian warehouse. As with its French flagship, the offerings are up-market. Covering five levels, you'll find everything that sets the heart of a sophisticated fashion devotee aflutter. In the basement is a gourmet department stocking an extensive range of French delicacies and wines.
friedrichstrasse 76-78, telephone 030 20 94 80, open mon-sat 10am-8pm, www.lafayette.de, u-bahnhof französische strasse

Nice to do

(5) Stroll around the **Tiergarten** (animal's garden), the biggest park in Berlin. It's located right between the Eastern and Western parts of the city and is a main meeting spot for Berliners. In summer, the park is packed with Turkish families barbecuing, and sports fans cycling, playing ball or exercising. It's a great place for an extensive walk and there are also small lakes on which to row. You won't see many wild animals here though; they were only around in the 19th century.

strasse des 17. juni, u-bahnhof zoologischer garten, s-bahnhof bellevue

(6) You may be familiar with this giant, golden goddess of victory from Wim Wenders' film 'Wings of Desire', in which the fallen angel, actor Bruno Ganz, sits on the goddess' shoulders. You can't climb as high as he does in the film, but you can get up to a round walk on top of **Siegessäule** (victory column), from which you can get a great view over Tiergarten park and the city.

grosser stern, strasse des 17. juni, telephone 030 391 29 61, open daily 9.30am-5pm, no admission, s-bahnhof tiergarten

(9) Take a lift in the **Hi Flyer balloon** for a splendid view over Berlin from a height of 150m. It's an unforgettable experience, but only for those who aren't afraid of heights.

potsdamer platz, no telephone, open daily 10am-10pm, admission €13, s-bahnhof potsdamer platz

Mitte South

Start your walk with a late breakfast, when Café Einstein ① is not too busy. From Einstein, walk down Unter den Linden towards the Brandenburg Gate and Pariser Platz. Walk through the Gate ② and turn right towards Reichstag ③. Expect a queue if you plan to get inside. If not, proceed to your right to Kanzleramt, where the chancellor resides. Continue ahead until you enter Tiergarten park on John-Foster-Dulles-Allee. After a few minutes you'll see the great Haus der Kulturen der Welt, where you can stop to watch exhibitions or pause for a coffee ④ on the terrace overlooking the Spree River. Continue ahead on John-Foster-Dulles-Allee ⑤ crossing through the Tiergarten Park. Ahead you'll see Schloß Bellevue, where the German president resides. Turn left into the park, walk ahead until you reach a big roundabout and you'll see the Siegessäule ⑥. Walk up the monument or cross Strasse des 17.Juni. Continue through the park on the other side of Strasse des 17.Juni until you reach the Kulturforum, with the Neue Nationalgalerie ⑦. Now you're close to Potsdamer Platz ⑧, and its cafés, shops and cinemas. Head to S-Bahnhof Potsdamer Platz ⑨ on Leipziger Strasse and continue until you pass the federal council on the right. When you reach Mauerstrasse, enter to the right. After a few meters, you'll reach Friedrichstrasse; continue until you reach Kochstrasse and Checkpoint Charlie ⑩. For a nice lunch, go to Sale e Tabacchi ⑪ or return to Friedrichstrasse, which you should follow north ⑫. Pass warehouses and lots of shops ⑬ ⑭ ⑮, then turn right on Französische Strasse, and again to the right or to the left on Charlottenstrasse. You are now on Gendarmenmarkt ⑲ where you can stroll around looking at the domes and concert halls. Choose from one of the cafés or adjoining restaurants ⑯ ⑰ ⑱. Return to Französische Strasse, where you should continue to the east. Pass the Werdersche Markt, where the foreign ministry is located. Continue until Spandauerstrasse, where you should turn right and enter the Nikolaiviertel, one of the few remnants of old Berlin, restored since GDR times. There you'll find restaurants ⑳ and cafés where you'll find excellent original Berlin food.

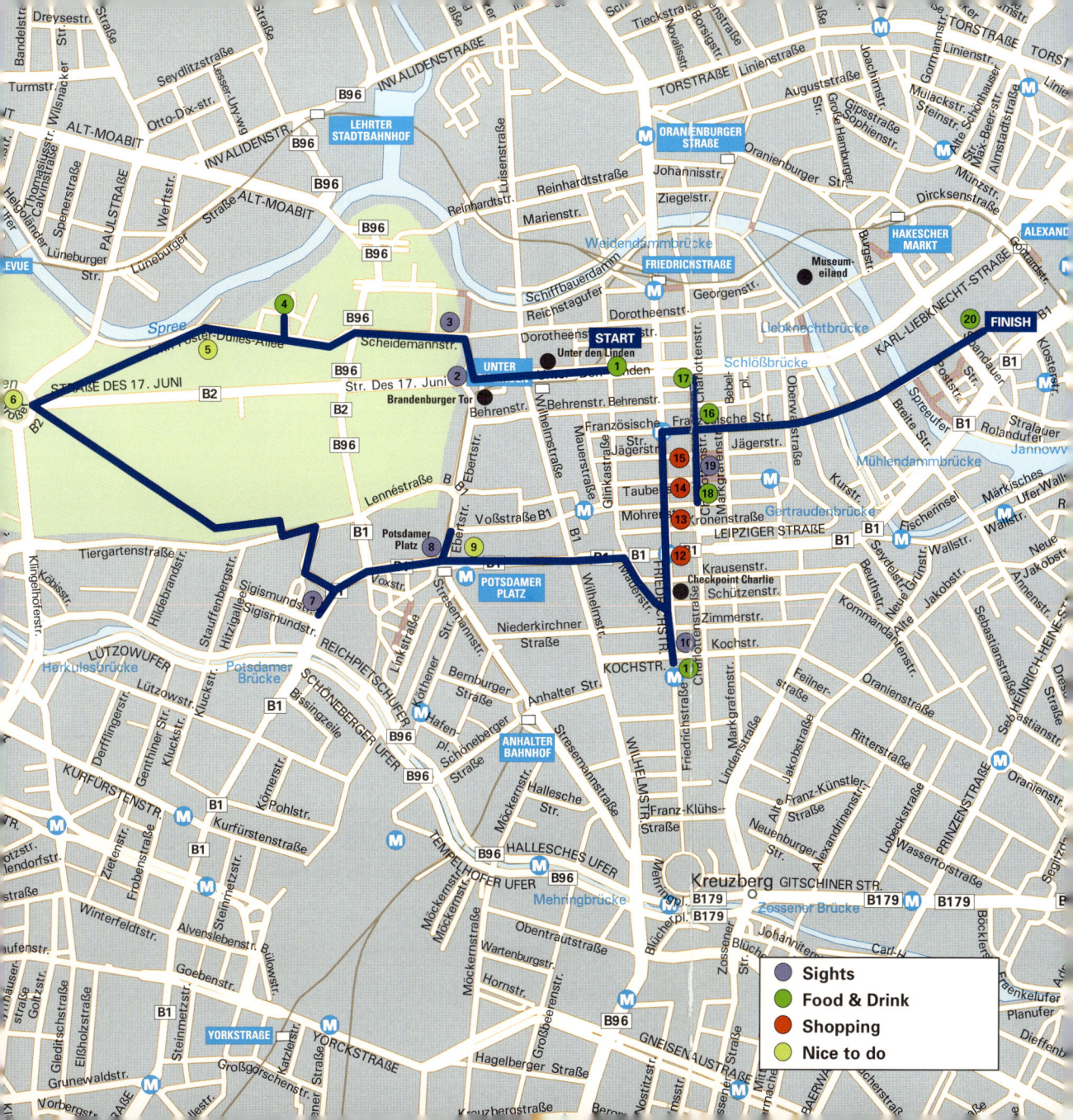

Sights

Food & Drink

Shopping

Nice to do

Kreuzberg 61

The southern part of Kreuzberg, called 'Kreuzberg 61' because of its former postal code, is the area where there's actually a 'cross hill' (Kreuzberg) after which the borough is named. The cross hill can be found in Viktoria Park, a nice little park with a fantastic view over Berlin. Nearby is Tempelhof airport, the former city airport that was built by the Nazis, one of the few surviving architectural records of the Third Reich.

- ● Sights
- ● Food & Drink
- ● Shopping
- ● Nice to do

4

Just a few blocks south lies Chamissoplatz, where there are still many old houses that survived World War II. Visit this area for a glimpse of pre-war Berlin. The nearby Bergmannstrasse area is the hub of neighborhood activity in '61', with shops, cafés and restaurants. Many of the places here haven't changed their location or their clientele since the Wall came down. Take a stroll through the Bergmannstrasse cemeteries, where you can see astonishingly luxurious crypts, illustrative of the city's former glory.

9 Musts!

Viktoria Luise Park

Get a great view of Berlin
from Kreuzberg Park

Airport Tempelhof

See Europe's
biggest building

Chamissoplatz

Take a trip back to
19th century Berlin

Z

Wine and dine
at this excellent
Greek restaurant

Raw Musique

Buy electronic music
from Berlin

Austria

Enjoy the best schnitzel
in town

Holzapfel

There's always a need
for a good knife

Casolare

Eat at the
punk rock pizzeria

Ankerklause

Meat the real Kreuzberg

 Sights

 Shopping

 **Food & drink**

Nice to do

VIKTORIA LUISE PARK ①

Sights

(1) **Viktoria Park** is where Kreuzbergers go on summer weekends to relax, enjoy the sun or cool their feet in the cheery, artificial waterfall. In winter, kids go sledding down the hill. At the top of the park stands Schinkel's monument commemorating the Prussian victories in the Napoleonic Wars, and from here there is a great view across the city. The cross on top of the hill gave Kreuzberg its name.
kreuzbergstrasse, open 24 hours, u-bahnhof platz der luftbrücke

(4) The **Chamissoplatz** is one of the most beautiful areas in Berlin. Here, you can get an impression of how the residential areas of Berlin must have looked before World War II. Many buildings in this neighborhood survived the wartime bombings, and the Chamissoplatz area has now been immaculately restored. Many films about 'old Berlin' were shot in the area.
chamissoplatz, u-bahnhof platz der luftbrücke

(17) The **Bergmannstrasse cemeteries** are huge, including four different linked areas. In summer, the cemeteries are great for quiet sunbathing - no children playing, no dogs and no music. Looking at the lavish gravestones and the incredibly big crypts is a reminder of how affluent Berlin once was. This is something you can't say of present Berlin, which is considered to be the poorest city in Germany. Many of the city's bourgeois elite (both German and Jewish) either fled or were killed during the Third Reich period, and much of the city was left in complete ruins after World War II. The following two and a half decades of division left deep scars in the social and economic structure of the city and pessimists say that Berlin will never recover the global significance it held at the turn of the 20th century. The Bergmannstrasse cemeteries are one place to catch a glimpse of the city's former glory.
bergmannstrasse, no telephone, open daily 7am-6pm, admission free, u-bahnhof südstern

⑳ The **Urbanhafen** used to be used as a trading harbor and is now a lake-like extension of one of the Spree River channels. From Admiralbrücke up to the West you'll have a beautiful view. Perfect for an after-dinner stroll.
urbanhafen, planufer, u-bahnhof schönleinstrasse

Food & Drink

(5) Sri Lankan delicacies are served up at **Chandra Kumari**, which offers many vegetarian meals, mostly using fresh, eco-friendly products. Not only is the food healthy, the prices are very modest too. If you are really hungry, order the wedding dish which comes with many dishes.
gneisenaustrasse 4, telephone 030 694 12 03, open daily noon-open end, price €8, u-bahnhof mehringdamm

(8) After you've wandered through Kreuzberg Park, Chamissoplatz and Bergmannstrasse, the **Milagro** is the perfect place to take a short rest and have a coffee or a second breakfast. At night, enjoy wholewheat pizza and tarte flambée. There's even a small side room for non-smokers, a rarity in a city like Berlin where smoking is very common amongst adults.
bergmannstrasse 12, telephone 030 692 23 03, open from 9am-1am, price €4, u-bahnhof gneisenaustrasse

(9) A real highlight on the always-busy Bergmannstrasse is the Japanese restaurant **Sumo**. With its super-stylish interior, it looks almost like trendy Mitte though the mixed Kreuzberg crowd inside doesn't seem to mind. Highly recommended are the sushi and the tuna steak served with rice. As a starter, try the steamed bean salad.
bergmannstrasse 89, telephone 030 69 00 49 63, open daily noon-midnight, price €8, u-bahnhof gneisenaustrasse

(13) **Z**, a little off Bergmannstrasse, is not a restaurant that you find by accident but because you are looking for good food and a nice atmosphere. The menu consists of Greek cooking with French and Italian influences, boasting classic grilled dishes as well as more innovative options like lamb with a balsamic honey sauce. If this all sounds too heavy for your stomach, choose one of the many types of Ouzo and just enjoy a drink. On weekends, Greek musicians make sure that the atmosphere is authentic and people often spontaneously begin to dance.
friesenstrasse 12, telephone 030 692 27 16, open daily 5pm-0.30am, price €10, u-bahnhof geneisenaustrasse

⑮ At cozy **Austria** you'll find the best schnitzels in Berlin. Be warned, however: they come in sizes almost as big as a pizza. They are so big, in fact, that you can easily share them or take the leftovers in a doggy bag. If you feel like a smaller portion, try the Kinderschnitzel (children's portion), which is also rich but more manageable. The other delicacies on the menu are worth trying: check out the lamb on ratatouille, which is equally delicious. Round out your meal with Austrian schnapps such as Marillenbrand or Pflaumenschnaps (plum schnapps). These will help with digestion. *bergmannstrasse 30, telephone 030 694 44 40, open daily 6pm-midnight, price €12, u-bahnhof zossenerstrasse*

⑱ **Delgados bar** is great for an early evening aperitif or cocktail. Try the minty Mojito or a tasty Daiquiri, mixed by bar owner Ferriols Delgado himself, and relax to the tunes that flow from the stereo. On Friday nights the Salsa parties are guaranteed to be grooving.
südstern 14, telephone 030 183 29 81, open tue-sun 5pm-open end, price €4, u-bahnhof südstern

⑲ The waiters at **Il Casolare** are all Italians, mostly charming, sometimes a little moody but always very quick. The pizzas here are crisp and thin and the homemade pasta is also fabulous. The posters of punk concerts and loud punk music that sometimes plays tell a lot about the restaurant's owners. Nevertheless, this is one of the most popular Italian restaurants in Berlin and the place is always busy, so make sure to reserve a table ahead. In summer, get a seat outside underneath the huge trees.
grimmstrasse 30, telephone 030 69 50 66 10, open daily noon-midnight, price €8, u-bahnhof schönleinstrasse

㉑ Small, always packed and a real Kreuzberg institution, the **Ankerklause** is a bar and café with history. Ever since this run-down corner pub with the charm of a harbor bar was taken over by young, aspiring barflies it has become one of Kreuzberg's premier nightspots. On Thursdays there's a dance party, and during the week you can have breakfast till 4pm and listen to reggae, indie rock or hip-hop.
maybachufer 1, telephone 030 693 56 49, open tue-sun 10am-4am, mon 4pm-4am, price €3, u-bahnhof schönleinstrasse

ÖFFNUNGSZEITEN
Di. - Sa. 09.00 - ?
So.   ?

DELGADOS BAR ⑱

Shopping

(6) When something's in good shape, it's **'In Bestform'** and that's what this shop is all about. Specializing in interior designs for the kitchen and bath, there are hundreds of different glasses, vases, pottery, and kitchen tools in steel, glass and plastic. No matter what type of taste you have, there is always something here that will look good in your home.
bergmannstrasse 8, telephone 030 694 03 99, open mon-wed 10am-7pm, thu-fri 10am-7.30pm, sat 10am-3pm, u-bahnhof gneisenaustrasse

(7) A couple of years ago, **Ararat** only carried postcards but now the range of products has been extended to stationery and small gifts and souvenirs. The postcards are still the best thing about this place though. Celebrities from film and music adorn the racks, and while Madonna, Elvis Presley and Marilyn Monroe were the leading stars for years, these days you'll also find lots of Britney Spears and Robbie Williams.
bergmannstrasse 99a, telephone 030 693 50 80, open mon-fri 10am-8pm, sat 10am-4pm, u-bahnhof gneisenaustrasse

(10) Comic fans shouldn't miss **Grober Unfug**, Berlin's leading comic store. From old-school funnies to the newest in Japanese mangas, this shop stocks a vast range of comic books, magazines, memorabilia and merchandising stuff from different fields of visual entertainment. There's also a large assortment of paraphernalia for sci-fi fans and every once in a while there is an exhibition in the shop.
zossenerstrasse 32-33, telephone 030 69 40 14 90, open mon-fri 11am-7pm, sat 11am-4pm, u-bahnhof gneisenaustrasse

(11) Electronic music in its various incarnations is available at **Raw** music, where you'll find original Berlin electronics, the latest in techno from Detroit and Drum 'n' Bass from the UK. New CDs and vinyls are available plus a nice selection of secondhand vinyl. The store's owners are music junkies, so if you are looking for a specific tune, just sing it to them and they will find it for you.
zossenerstrasse 20, telephone 030 694 78 15, open mon-fri 1pm-8pm, u-bahnhof gneisenaustrasse

(12) Horst-Dieter Schmahl's **Radio Art** is one of the most curious shops in Berlin. He has a collection of hundreds of old radios and other electronic devices from the past. As an engineer, he knows how to repair old stuff so if you have some old technology to fix, bring it in and Schmahl will do anything he can to get it functioning again.

zossenerstrasse 2, telephone 030 693 94 35, open mon-fri 1pm-6pm, u-bahnhof gneisenaustrasse

(14) **Hammett** stocks over 5000 crime titles in German and over 1000 books in English. Collectors will find many sought-after titles, and if you are looking for that special book, Hammett's Claudia Denker will easily be able to help you. She seems to have read every book she stocks, which is something you likely can't say for the people working in the big media warehouses in Mitte.

friesenstrasse 27, telephone 030 691 58 34, open mon-fri 11am-8pm, sat 11.00-15.00, u-bahnhof gneisenaustrasse

(16) **Holzapfel** has the most amazing range of knives in stock. Whether it's hand-made Japanese knives or hard U.S. blades, saws and axes, Holzapfel has the sharpest stuff around. For the passionate cook or amateur carpenter, Holzapfel is a must.

bergmannstrasse 25, telephone 030 78 99 06 10, open mon-fri 11am-7pm, sat 11.00-14.30, u-bahnhof gneisenaustrasse

HOLZAPFEL ⑯

Nice to do

(2) The giant **Tempelhof airport** was once the central city airport. Built in the 1920s, it was greatly expanded by the Nazis and is one of the biggest buildings in the world. During the Berlin airlift in 1948-49, U.S. planes landed here to bring supplies to the blockaded city. The monument in front of the main building commemorates those years. Today, the airport is mainly used for domestic and small international flights. When you travel from Berlin, always make sure you mention name of the airport you'd like to go. With three airports in Berlin, taxi drivers sometimes get confused.
platz der luftbrücke, telephone 030 18 05 00 01 86 www.berlin-airport.de, open daily 5.30am-9pm, no admission, u-bahnhof platz der luftbrücke

(3) Opened in 1998 in a former cinema for U.S. forces, the **Columbia Fritz** hosts one of the most popular stages for live music, especially for independent rock music. Check the program on www.columbiafritz.de - there's a concert almost every day. In summer, there are swings and beach seats in the adjoining summer garden.
columbiadamm 9-11, telephone 030 698 12 80, www.columbiafritz.de, admission varies, u-bahnhof platz der luftbrücke

(22) The **'Turkish market'** on Maybachufer is definitely worth a visit. On Tuesdays and Fridays the market features exotic food, from ripe mangos to all sorts of oriental spices, breads and vegetables. Right before the stalls close, you can make deals with the vendors getting, for example, a box of avocados for the price of three single ones.
maybachufer, telephone 030 781 58 44, u-bahnhof schönleinstrasse

Kreuzberg 61

Walk up to Viktoria Park ① for the great view of Berlin from the Schinkel monument at its peak. Walk down the hill onto Methfesselstrasse, pass the freshly restored Viktoriaquarter, which used to be a brewery and now hosts exquisite apartments. Continue to Dudenstrasse, then turn left and walk towards Platz der Luftbrücke and cross the square until you stand in front of Tempelhof airport ② to get an impression of the typical neo-classicist Nazi architecture, of which the main hall of Tempelhof airport is one of the few remaining original buildings in the city. Either stroll around the airport or take one of the guided tours or continue down on Columbiadamm ③, until you reach Friesenstrasse. Walk past the red brick Columbushaus, a former prison that is now home to the Berlin police department, then turn left on Alexisstrasse until you reach Chamissoplatz ④. Walk down Nositzstrasse to Bergmannstrasse ⑤ ⑥ ⑦ ⑧ ⑨, which is a nice place for a stroll. Have a look at the shops and cafés, maybe take a break for lunch or coffee, then continue until you reach Zossenerstrasse on the left. Walk down ⑩ ⑪ ⑫ and return. Continue at the Bergmannstrasse again until you reach Friesenstrasse ⑬ ⑭ and return. Turn right and to the left you'll reach the Markthalle (market hall) and the Marheinekeplatz. Pass the Passionskirche to the left of the Bergmannstrasse ⑮ ⑯ and continue till you reach the entrance to the Bergmannstrasse cemeteries ⑰. When you reach the cemetery of Kirchhof Jerusalem, return to Bergmannstrasse. Turn right to the Südstern and its church. If it's already late afternoon, make a quick stop at Delgados Bar ⑱ for an aperitif or light drink. Continue on Körtestrasse, cross Urbanstrasse and the residential areas until you reach Il Casolare ⑲, where you should have late lunch or early dinner. Make sure to call on the way to reserve a table. After you've eaten, take a walk around Urbanhafen ⑳ or go for another drink to the right alongside Planufer ㉑. If it's still afternoon, check out the Turkish Market ㉒, which is always worth a visit.

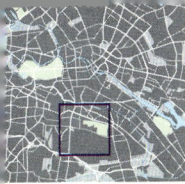

Charlottenburg & Wilmersdorf

The boroughs of Charlottenburg and Wilmersdorf were, during the 70s and 80s, the heart of West Berlin. Tourists arrived by train at the Zoo central station, stayed at Kurfürstendamm hotels and went shopping in the same area. In the evening, the theaters and cinemas around the Zoo area attracted tourists and Berliners alike.

- Sights
- Food & Drink
- Shopping
- Nice to do

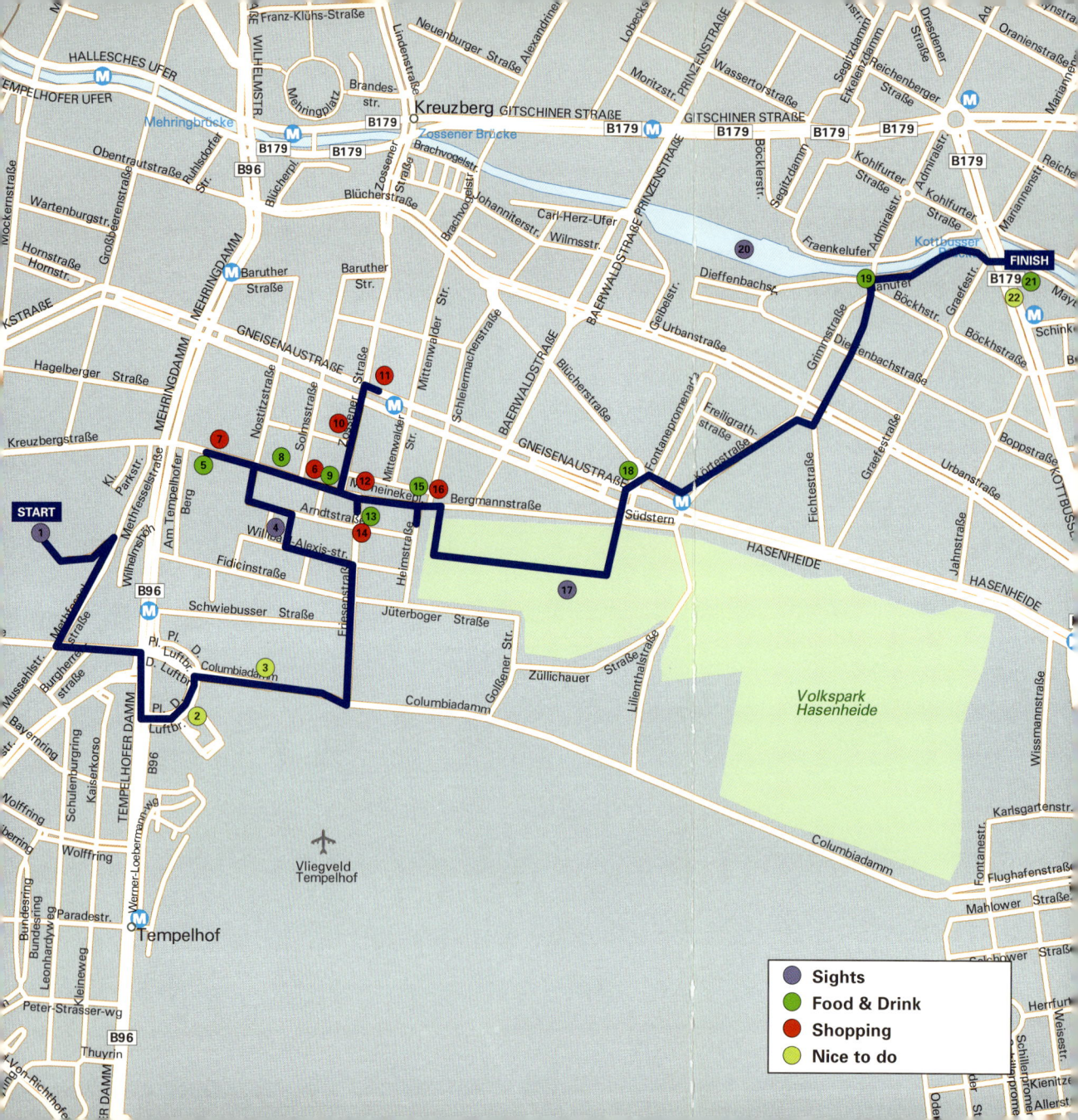

5

Contemporary Charlottenburg still has a lot of appeal. The Zoo and the shopping area, with department stores like KaDeWe, as well as the Kurfürstendamm (simply called 'Ku Damm' by locals) are worth a visit. Soak up more atmosphere around the areas of Savignyplatz, Bleibtreustrasse and Kantstrasse, where you'll find some of the most exquisite shops and best restaurants in Berlin. (Charlottenburg is where many of Berlin's affluent citizens live.) Even though the heart of the city beats in other boroughs these days, Charlottenburg maintains a dominant position in the city's commercial and cultural life.

9 Musts!

Zoologischer Garten

Have a stroll through this park and don't miss the aquarium

KaDeWe

Enter shopper's paradise, continental Europe's largest warehouse

Witty's

Enjoy an original Berlin 'wurst'

Stilwerk

Design fans love this temple of style

Paris Bar

Dine with Hollywood actors

Zwölf Apostel

Pizza fans...get happy!

Butter Lindner

Shop for Berlin delicacies and dairy products

Art & Industry

Find top-quality used designer clothing

Schildhorn Antiquitäten

Have a look at one of Berlin's finest antique shops

 Sights

 Shopping

 Food & drink

○ **Nice to do**

LUDWIG-KIRCH ㉑

Sights

(2) Built in 1848, the **Zoologischer Garten** is one of the oldest zoos in Germany and you won't have to walk long distances to see the animals. Watch the gorillas striking a pose, inspect insects of all kinds, see hippos gliding through water and behold the famous Berlin pandas. The aquarium displays sea animals and fish of all kinds - including sharks!
hardenbergplatz 8, telephone 030 25 40 10, www.zoo-berlin.de, open daily 9.30am-6pm, admission zoo or aquarium €9 adults and €4,50 children, zoo+aquarium €14 adults, €7 children, u & s-bahnhof zoologischer garten

(8) At **Savignyplatz** there are dozens of small shops of all kinds, including bookshops, fashion boutiques, shops for interior design and delicacy markets. Stroll around the square and you'll find it all. Even if shopping isn't your thing, this is a nice square to walk through. On weekends, Charlottenburg's locals promenade here or sit in one of the many cafés and restaurants.
savignyplatz, s-bahnhof savignyplatz

(21) **Ludwig-Kirch-Platz** is especially great in summer. Its many street cafés and small shops give you a feeling of being in Paris. See for yourself.
ludwig-kirch-platz, u-bahnhof hohenzollernplatz

(23) Many of the streets in Schöneberg end at **Viktoria-Luise-Platz**, a square with a big fountain at its center. The surrounding cafés and restaurants are very popular amongst Schönebergers and Charlottenburgers, who stroll around the square with their kids on the weekends.
viktoria-luise-platz, u-bahnhof viktoria-luise-platz

⑤ **SCHWARZES CAFÉ**

Food & Drink

(1) **Schleusenkrug** is always busy, as it is one of the only beer gardens in Tiergarten. In the summertime it is quite hard to get a seat, even though the garden is huge. But be patient, because it's worth the wait. There are few places where you can so easily rub shoulders with a mixed crowd of Berliners enjoying a beer and some grilled meat. In winter, Schleusenkrug is very cozy and not as busy and on weekends there are dance parties, mostly with 'easy listening' music.

müller-breslau-strasse 10, telephone 030 313 99 09, open mon-fri 10am-1am, sat-sun 10am-3am, price €3, s-bahnhof zoologischer garten

(4) **Witty's** is right across from KaDeWe - in case you didn't grab a snack in the warehouse's huge delicacy department. Witty's sausages are made from organically raised cattle - an eco-friendly fast food stand! Even the fries have a 'bio food' tag on them and are fried in fat that is changed daily. The price for these delights is higher than average but you'll immediately taste the difference.

wittenbergplatz, telephone 030 853 70 55, open 11am-1am, price €2.50, u-bahnhof wittenbergplatz

(5) The **Schwarzes Café** is a West Berlin classic that has been around since the late 1970s. Very popular amongst tourists and night clubbers, it's one of the few spots in Charlottenburg where you can get something warm to eat 24 hours a day, whether it's breakfast or a wholesome meat dish. Be patient with your orders, however, as the waiters are sometimes a bit confused.

kantstrasse 148, telephone 030 313 80 38, open daily 24 hours, price €6, s-bahnhof savignyplatz

(6) The **Paris Bar** is probably one of the most famous restaurants in Germany, not so much because of its food but because there's not one square centimeter that hasn't been touched by a celebrity, be it Madonna, Robert de Niro or Mikhail Gorbachev. The Paris Bar is indeed where people go to see and be seen. The food on the French menu is quite good, as are the waiters, with whom you should speak French if you want to get a table when the place is full. Start your evening with an aperitif at the Bar du Paris next door, which serves excellent Bellinis and good champagne.
kantstrasse 152, telephone 030 313 80 52, open daily noon-2am, price €20, u-bahnhof uhlandstrasse

(10) Great for sitting out on the street in summer, the **Aedes Café** is known as a good place to watch people as they pass the railway arches. Grab coffee, breakfast or one of the small dishes on the menu.
savignyplatz, s-bahn bogen 599, telephone 030 315 095 35, open daily 9am-1am, price €4, s-bahnhof savignyplatz,

(11) **Zwölf Apostel** is so popular that it has two other branches in the eastern part of the city. The marble floor and paintings on the ceiling give it a proper Italian ambiance, while the light is dim and a piano player performs at night. But it's the stone oven pizzas - made 24 hours a day - that have made the restaurant so famous. Some say they're the best in town. If you're hungry, try Monday's all-you-can-eat Pizza Party.
bleibtreustrasse 49, telephone 030 312 14 33, open daily 24 hours, price €8, s-bahnhof savignyplatz

(13) For artists and art lovers, **Lubitsch** is the place. During Berlinale this restaurant is packed, but it's a popular meeting spot for the art crowd at any time of year. The food is basic but very tasty and the atmosphere is unrushed and distinguished.
bleibtreustrasse 47, telephone 030 882 37 56, open mon-fri 9.30am-1am, sun 6pm-1am, price €12, u-bahnhof uhlandstrasse

(14) With its cobblestone pavement, antique interior and vine-entwined inner yard, the **Zillemarkt** seems like an old market hall. The food on the menu is almost as traditional as the interior and guests enjoy basic German meals and various sorts of draft beer at modest prices. This place is popular amongst residents and tourists alike.
bleibtreustrasse 48a, telephone 030 881 70 40, open daily 10am-1am, price €8, u-bahnhof savignyplatz

(17) The Croissanterie **Beloous** is great for a quick snack or a authentic French café au lait and is the place to get French baguettes, pastry and, of course, croissants - all baked in-house. Forget Starbucks and the other coffee chain stores you'll find on Ku'Damm. At this croissanterie, you can expect quality. No wonder people from all over Charlottenburg come here to buy their bread, coffee and breakfast rolls.
pariser strasse 23-24, telephone 030 883 27 33, open mon-fri 10am-7pm, open sat 10am-2pm, price €2, u-bahnhof uhlandstrase

(24) The terrace of **Montevideo** offers a lovely view of beautiful Viktoria-Luise-Platz. Enjoy an ice cream, coffee or, in the afternoon, a nice piece of cake. By the way, the café's name has nothing to do with Uruguay.
viktoria luise platz 6, telephone 030 213 10 20, open mon-sat 8am-1am, sun 9am-1am, price €4, u-bahnhof viktoria-luise-platz

Shopping

(3) **KaDeWe** stands for Kaufhaus des Westens and during the time of the Berlin Wall this department store was the ultimate symbol of Western capitalism and consumer culture. Even today, you can find everything at KaDeWe. From fine garments to designer TVs and a delicacy department with 1300 kinds of cheese and 1200 types of sausages, KaDeWe carries it all. This is Berlin's answer to Harrods and Macy's and is definitely worth a visit.

tauentzienstrasse 21-24, telephone 030 212 10, open mon-fri 9.30am-8pm, sat 9.00am-4pm, u-bahnhof wittenbergplatz

(7) Charlottenburg is known for its many interior design stores. If you're not in the mood to stroll around, head straight for **Stilwerk**, the luxurious answer to chains like Habitat or Ikea. This mall, with over 52 individual stores, carries almost everything a style-conscious buyer can think of, from kitchen and bathroom devices to lamps, glass and wood.

kantstrasse corner uhlandstrasse, telephone 030 315 150, open mon-fri 10am-8pm, sat 10am-4pm, s-bahnhof savignyplatz

(9) At **Riccardo Cortillone**, new styles of Italian shoes arrive every other week. You'll always find the latest in Italian shoe fashions, for both men and women. Across the street, is a store for bargains, (shoes from last season or former display pairs). With these shoes, you're 'always in style', just like Mink De Ville used to sing.

savignyplatz 4, telephone 030 312 97 01, open mon-fri 10am-8pm, sat 10am-4pm, s-bahnhof savignyplatz

(12) **L'Orange** stocks pret-a-porter-fashion from young French companies. Although you won't find well-known designer names here, women will find elegant yet edgy basics. The shop is bright and colorful with French pop-musique playing, and if you are a Francophile you can even speak French with the employees.

bleibtreustrasse 5a, telephone 030 315 048 83, open mon-fri 10am-8pm, sat 10am-4pm, s-bahnhof savignyplatz

RICARDO CORTILLONE ⑨

(15) In Charlottenburg, women always dress a little better than in other parts of the city. When they eventually get tired of their dresses, jewelry and shoes they give them to **Chiara**. This second-hand shop is where to find top brands and designers. You might see 1970's Chanel shoes window display, or vintage YSL on the racks and, if you are lucky, grab an original Prada bag from the early 1980s.
bleibtreustrasse 39, telephone 030 886 806 71, open mon-fri 11am-7pm, sat 11am-4pm, s-bahnhof savignyplatz

(16) **Art & Industry** is for furniture lovers. From art deco to Bauhaus, 1950s classics to colorful 1970s designs, this shop presents selected objects, single pieces and groups of 20th century furniture from Germany, Italy, Scandinavia and the US. If you haven't been to a museum of interior design lately, drop by Art & Industry. It's practically the same experience, with only one difference: everything here is for sale.
bleibtreustrasse 40, telephone 030 883 49 36, open mon-fri 2pm-6.30pm, sat 11am-4 pm, s-bahnhof savignyplatz

(18) **Butter Lindner** is a Berlin-based chain that is best known for its high-quality dairy products. Try the delicious salted butter or the fantastic fruit yogurt. Also highly recommended are Butter Lindner's cakes and their selection of whole wheat breads.
ludwig-kirch-strasse 11, telephone 030 886 295 90, open mon-fri 10am-7pm, sat 10am-4pm, u-bahnhof uhlandstrasse

(19) **Zigarren Herzog** is quiet, dark, cool and a little humid - the perfect atmosphere for storing and selecting cigars. At Herzog's you can even store your precious purchases in private lockers that can be rented. There's a smoker's room too, where you can enjoy a quality smoke with a glass of single malt whiskey or Bordeaux. Of course you can also walk out with one of the world's finest cigars, or an exclusive cigar accessory.
ludwig-kirch-platz 1, telephone 030 886 823 40, open mon-fri 10am-8pm, sat 10am-4pm, u-bahnhof uhlandstrasse

(20) **Schildhorn Antiquitäten** stocks late 19th-century and Art Deco furniture. Don't miss it… this shop is a must-see for anyone even slightly interested in this style of furniture. The owner, Anke-Friederike Michaelsen, stocks rare and unusual pieces from all over the world, with a focus on Scandinavia, England and France. Glasses, lamps, mirrors, vases, silver, beautiful chairs and small tables - this store is full of such wonderful things it is hard to mention them all. Occasionally, the shop opens its storage facilities and sells some items at half price. Call to find out when.

ludwig-kirch-platz 2, telephone 030 883 10 34, open mon-fri 2pm-6.30pm, sat 11am-2pm, u-bahnhof uhlandstrasse

(22) **Coledampf's** is colloquial German for having an enormous appetite - an apt name for a store that carries the utensils a cook's heart will beat for. The shop has stainless steel and aluminum pots in all sizes, directly imported from Italy and Scandinavia. They look so nice that it's hard to leave without buying one. So why resist… couldn't your kitchen use another good pot?

uhlandstrasse 54-55, telephone 030 883 91 91, open mon-fri 10am-8pm, sat 10am-4pm, u-bahnhof uhlandstrasse

coledampf's
CulturCentrum

Jetzt wird's BUNT!

Charlottenburg & Wilmersdorf

A good walk to start after breakfast. This walk takes you through the West Berlin of the time of the wall, with its nice squares, exquisite shops and restaurants. Start your walk at Schleusenkrug ① with a coffee, then head towards Zoologischer Garten ②. If you fancy watching animals, enter the park; if not, turn left at Zoo station towards Gedächtniskirche, pass the Asian entrance of the Zoo. Turn left on the Budapester Strasse, pass the Europa Center, then turn right on Nürnberger Strasse and continue till you reach Tauentzienstrasse. Turn left and head for KaDeWe ③, where you can stroll for a couple of hours. Cross the street for a bio-sausage snack ④, then walk west down Tauentzienstrasse, turn right at Joachimsthaler Strasse, then left and enter Kantstrasse. If you feel like a coffee, stop at Schwarzes Café ⑤, or continue down Kantstrasse ⑥ ⑦ till you reach Savignyplatz ⑧ ⑨ ⑩ ⑪. Walk toward the rails and enter the passage to Bleibtreustrasse. Turn right for L'Orange ⑫ or left for some food ⑬ ⑭ or second-hand shopping ⑮. Take the second right to Mommsenstrasse ⑯, then left on Wielandstrasse, cross Ku'damm again, go left and go to the right to Schlüter-strasse. Continue till Pariserstrasse ⑰, ⑱ till you enter Ludwig-Kirch-Strasse and carry on until you reach Ludwig-Kirch-Platz ⑲ ⑳ ㉑ ㉒. Cross Uhland-strasse and continue on Schaperstrasse through a nice residential area until you reach Nürnberger Platz. Cross it and continue on Geisbergstrasse. When you reach Ansbacher Strasse, you've almost reached the tour's end. Walk down to the next street, Winterfeldstrasse, turn left and you are at Viktoria-Luise-Platz ㉓, where you can relax your feet on one of the benches at the square, or with a nice coffee ㉔ at one of the square's cafés. If you're taking public transport, turn left for the subway stop U-Bahnhof Viktoria-Luise-Platz.

Kreuzberg 36, Treptow & Friedrichshain

Twenty years ago, Kreuzberg was the center for Berlin's alternative culture. In the 1970s and 80s this area, enclosed on two sides by the Wall, was full of squatters, punks and Turkish immigrants attracted by the low or non-existent rents. These days, although the squats have vanished and the alternative scene has moved towards Prenzlauer Berg or Friedrichshain, you can still sense that rebellious feeling in Kreuzberg.

On Oranienstrasse there are plenty of cafés, restaurants, bars and clubs worth visiting. Very close to Oranienstrasse, at Kottbusser Tor, is the heart

- Sights
- **Food & Drink**
- **Shopping**
- Nice to do

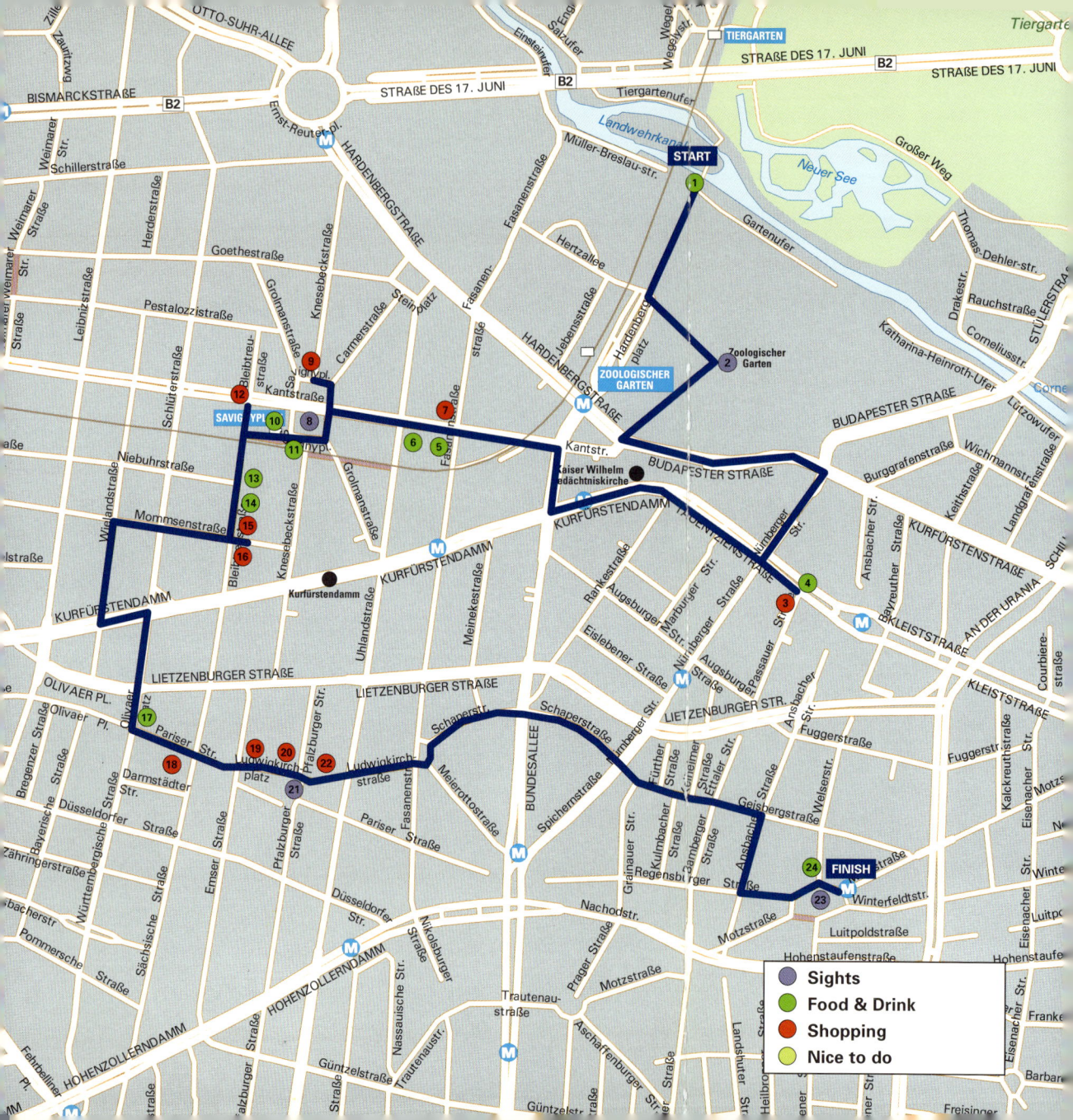

6

of Turkish Berlin - filled with kebab shops, bars and Turkish travel agents. Off Oranienstrasse lies Görlitzer Park, where Kreuzberg's populace meets for barbecues and ball games in the summer.

Towards Treptow are the beautiful Treptower Park and the giant Soviet war memorial. Heading back to the Spree River, it isn't far to the Oberbaum-brücke where you can cross from Kreuzberg to Friedrichshain. Nearby is the longest remaining stretch of the Berlin Wall, now called the East Side Gallery.

9 Musts!

Hasir

Get a taste of
Turkish Berlin

Melek Pastanesi

Experience German
Turkish fusion

Die Imaginäre Manufaktur

Buy handmade basketry

Görlitzer Park

See the Kreuzberg
mix of people

Freischwimmer

Dine by the river

Sowjetische Ehrendenkmal Treptow

Stroll through the park
and look at
the monument

Oberbaumbrücke

Get great views
of Mitte

Fritz Fischer

Choose from the
big fish selection
and admire the Spree

East Side Gallery

See the longest
remaining stretch
of the Berlin wall

 Sights
Shopping

  Food & drink
Nice to do

Sights

(12) In the summer, Kreuzberg's residents hang out in **Görlitzer Park**.
Kids romp in the playground or play with animals at the 'kinder farm'
while adults barbecue an entire sheep or pig, lie lazily in the sun or enjoy
an occasional open air concert. During winter, the park is great for jogging.
skalitzer strasse, open 24 hours daily, u-bahnhof görlitzer bahnhof

(13) Thousands of Russian soldiers died in World War II's battle for Berlin.
Sowjetische Ehrendenkmal in Treptower Park commemorates the fallen
with a huge and sobering monument. At the end of a tree-lined avenue is
the statue of Mother Russia weeping for her lost sons. At the far end of the
memorial is a huge statue of a Soviet soldier holding a child in one arm and
destroying the Swastika with the other. Not to be missed, this is a lovely
place for a Sunday afternoon stroll at any time of year.
treptower park/puschkinallee, s-bahnhof treptower park

(17) The **Oberbaumbrücke** received its name in the late 18th century when
it was a Customs point for boats on the Spree. During the division of the
city, the Oberbaumbrücke was a border crossing between East and West
Berlin. Today, cars, pedestrians and the subway cross the red brick bridge,
from which there is a fantastic view over the Spree towards Mitte and the
heart of Berlin.
warschauer strasse/skalitzer strasse, u & s-bahnhof warschauer strasse

④ **MELEK PASTANESI**

Food & Drinks

(1) **Hasir** is considered to have the best 'Döner Kebabs' in Berlin. (Döner is a pita bread pocket stuffed with roasted meat, invented in Berlin by Turkish immigrants.) At Hasir, Döners are fresh, served with a special sauce and cost only €2. Many Turks frequent this restaurant day and night - what better sign that the food is excellent? Don't leave Berlin without trying one.
adalbertstrasse 10, telephone 030 614 23 73, open daily 24 hours, price €2, u-bahnhof kottbusser tor

(2) **Max & Moritz** is named after two famous characters by German illustrator Wilhelm Busch, considered one of the first comic artists to emerge in the early 20th century. At this restaurant, which has the atmosphere of an old tavern, wholesome Berlin food is on the menu. The huge portions might be hard to handle but the food is delicious. Try Königsberger Klopse, stuffed cabbage or one of the Braten, roasted meats that come with delicious sauces. By the way, all the meat is top-quality and comes from eco-friendly farms outside Berlin. On Sundays there's tango dancing from 6pm.
oranienstrasse 162, telephone 030 695 159 11, open daily from noon-whenever, price €10, u-bahnhof kottbusser tor

(4) **Melek Pastanesi** is a bakery that sells both German and Turkish breads and sweets. 'Dürums' are sold here alongside Berlin specialties like 'Berliner Pfannkuchen' (pancake), while pita bread sits next to German rolls. This is multiculturalism at its best and the shop is open 24 hours a day.
oranienstrasse 28, telephone 030 614 51 86, open daily 24 hours, price €2, u-bahnhof kottbusser tor

⑤ The **Bierhimmel** (beer heaven) is a 1950s-style bar popular during the day with an interesting mix of 'Kiez' people (Berlin slang for neighborhood people). At night, the Bierhimmel becomes a hetero-friendly gay and lesbian bar. The list of beers is, despite the name, not impressive though - it's a remnant of a former pub located here that only used to serve beer.

oranienstrasse 183, telephone 030 615 31 22, open daily 1pm-3am, price €3, u-bahnhof kottbusser tor

⑥ Standing outside **Amrit**, you can smell the Indian spices the cook deftly uses on his food. Amongst Kreuzbergers, this is one of the most popular restaurants around. The food is delicious, the service is always friendly and the prices are great. It might be a bit noisy for a romantic rendezvous, but it's perfect for any other occasion.

oranienstrasse 202-203, telephone 030 612 55 50, open sun-thu noon-1am, fri-sat noon-2am, price €6, u-bahnhof görlitzer bahnhof

⑦ The **Bateau Ivre**, named after a poem by Arthur Rimbaud, is a French coffee house that attracts Kreuzberg artists and neighbors looking for a good, strong coffee during the day. At night the place comes alive, serving food such as cold tapas plates and delicious French cakes. The friendly and flirtatious atmosphere attracts the cream of Kreuzberg's 20- and 30-somethings. Join them!

oranienstrasse 18, telephone 030 614 036 59, open sun-thu 9am-2pm, fri-sat 9am-4am, price € 7, u-bahnhof kottbusser tor

(10) **Madonna bar** is known for serious, rock-and-roll style drinking. The whiskey list contains 250 options, carefully selected by the bar's owner (who is a passionate collector). Look at the ceiling while downing your drink - there's a funny fresco referring to the seven deadly sins, a perfect fit with the loud rock music that always plays over the bar's sound system.
wiener strasse 22, telephone 030 611 69 43, open daily 3pm-open end, price €5, u-bahnhof görlitzer strasse

(11) If you crave vegetarian food after midnight, make **Café V** your destination. The meatless cooking includes pizzas, salads and daily selections such as mushrooms on tofu or broccoli with yogurt sauce. Yummy and healthy food at decent prices - what a treat!
lausitzer platz 12, telephone 030 612 45 05, open daily 10am-2pm, price €8, u-bahnhof görlitzer strasse

(15) **Freischwimmer** is fabulous for outdoor dining in warm weather and cozy and warm in winter. Located in what used to be a small boat harbor, diners sit alongside the Spree channel. The crowd is young and hip and the menu is international, ranging from Jamaican appetizers to fish & chips. On Sundays, Freischwimmer offers a huge brunch buffet.
vor dem schlesischen tor 2, telephone 030 610 743 09, open mon-fri noon-whenever, sat-sun 11am-whenever, price €8, u-bahnhof schlesisches tor

⑯ **Mysliwska** means 'hunter's place' in Polish. Despite its weird name, this bar has been popular amongst artistic people for more than a decade. Czech Budweiser on tap, good music and friendly service ensure that it is always crowded. The formerly industrial surrounding area of Schlesisches Tor has recently become very trendy as media companies have moved in, so expect media mavens of all types at the bar ending their long work day with a beer and a chat.

schlesische strasse 35, telephone 030 611 48 60, open daily 6pm-whenever, u-bahnhof schlesisches tor

⑱ **Fritz Fischer** quickly established itself as one of the best fish restaurants in Berlin soon after its opening in 2002. Besides the exquisite fish, the menu also contains delicious vegetarian meals as well as an impressive list of wines. Dinner guests also receive free admission to the 12 34 club, upstairs from the restaurant. Fritz Fischer is located on the ground floor of the Universal Music building.

stralauer allee 1, telephone 030 520 07 22 02, open mon-sat 11.30am-3pm, 6.30pm-whenever, price €18, u & s-bahnhof warschauer strasse

Shopping

(3) At **Die Imaginäre Manufaktur**, blind people weave baskets from unusual materials. Under the supervision of Berlin designers Vogt+Weizenegger, the Imaginäre Manufaktur builds magazine racks and mirror frames from brushes and coat hangers from baskets. The end results are practical, everyday goods with a highly individualistic edge.
oranienstrasse 26, telephone 030 25 88 66 14, open mon-wed 9am-5pm, thu 10am-6pm, fri 9am-3pm, u-bahnhof kottbusser tor

(8) **Grüne Papeterie** stocks unusual stationery at excellent prices. You'll find paper made from flowers, hand-made paper from Tibet, photo albums, hand-made leather desk accessories and beautiful wrapping paper.
oranienstrasse 196, telephone 030 618 53 55, open mon-fri 10am-7.30pm, sat 10am-4pm, u-bahnhof kottbusser tor

(9) At **Modern Graphics** the comic book is king. From mangas to adventure games to American superheroes, Modern Graphic stocks it all. Check out the do-it-yourself manga books, which advise aspiring artists on how to draw in real manga style.
oranienstrasse 22, telephone 030 615 88 10, open mon-thu 10am-6.30pm, fri 10am-8pm, sat 10am-4pm, u-bahnhof kottbusser tor

DIM
DIE IMAGINÄRE MANUFAKTUR

Nice to do

(14) From May until late August, fans of Caribbean music meet at **Yaam** for various open-air activities. Get in on a pick-up basketball game or just soak up the sun and enjoy some original Jamaican cooking while the DJ plays reggae, soca and hip-hop. Sundays are the busiest days at Yaam, when you can get started on your caipirinhas at 2pm - a great way to see Berlin's more colorful side.

eichenstrasse 4, telephone 030 615 13 54, www.yaam.de, admission €4, u-bahnhof schlesisches tor

(19) Aside from a few spots in Mitte, namely in Zimmerstrasse and Bernauer Strasse, the longest remaining stretch of the former Berlin Wall is alongside Mühlenstrasse. Stretching over a kilometer, the wall is now known as the **East Side Gallery** because of the dozens of colorful paintings that cover the concrete blocks. Not only is this a nice place for a walk, it's also great for taking photos and for musing over what an absurd piece of architecture the wall was.

mühlenstrasse, www.berliner-mauer.de, u-bahnhof warschauer strasse

Kreuzberg 36, Treptow & Friedrichshain

This tour will take you through Kreuzberg 36 to Treptow and to the fringes of Friedrichshain. Start around lunchtime since Kreuzberg wakes up late and its shops and cafés normally don't open before 11am or noon. Begin at the heart of Kreuzberg 61 on Adalbertstrasse ① or with a nice plate of Sauerkraut and Wurst around the corner on Oranienstrasse ②. In the 1980s, this used to be the hippest street in Berlin but it has now lost its edge as young people have begun to explore the Eastern boroughs. Kreuzberg has still maintained its alternative charm, however, with the Oranienstrasse being its main street. Have a look at the shops, cafés and restaurants ③ ④ ⑤ ⑥ ⑦ ⑧ ⑨ as you head towards Görlitzer Bahnhof. Follow the Oranienstrasse, which then turns into Wienerstrasse ⑩. To wine and dine at Café V ⑪, turn left on Lausitzer Strasse and head for Lausitzer Platz. If you want to hang out in the green, proceed on Wienerstrasse until you reach Görlitzer Park ⑫, through which you can stroll until you've reached Görlitzer Ufer. Turn left and proceed until you reach Heckmannufer. The next street you reach is Schlesische Strasse. Turn right and keep walking down the alley, with its beautiful trees, until it turns into Puschkinallee. Continue and then turn right when you see Treptower Park, where you'll find the Soviet commemoration monument ⑬. To return to town, walk back to Am Treptower Park Street and go back to Schlesische Strasse. After the extensive walk through the park you might need a rest. When Am Treptower Park Street hits Puschkinallee, you'll see Eichenstrasse. At the end of this street you'll find Yaam ⑭ on the left. If you want something quieter, continue on Am Treptower Park for Freischwimmer ⑮, which is between the channel and the gas station. For a quick beer try Mysliwska ⑯. After your break, continue on Schlesische Strasse until you reach Schlesisches Tor, then turn right and walk alongside the rails until you reach Oberbaumbrücke ⑰. If you're hungry, turn right for Fritz Fischer ⑱. If you want to see remains of the Berlin wall turn left on Mühlenstrasse ⑲ and walk down the always-congested street.

Ⓜ Although it is an autonomous city, **Potsdam** is often considered the most beautiful part of Berlin. For centuries it was the place where the Prussian power elite lived; its kings built huge parks and beautiful rococo castles in the surrounding area of Potsdam. These weren't destroyed in World War II and have recently been restored. From the Sanssoussi castle to the Orangerie, Potsdam offers more than 400 years of Prussian history. A definite must for every Berlin visitor, there are numerous tours through Potsdam. One of the nicest is the 'Alter Fritz Radwanderweg', which allows you to see the sights while riding a rented bike. Check out *www.potsdam.de* to see where you can rent the bikes and visit www.spsg.de for a look at the opening hours of the parks and castles, which change throughout the year. *s-bahnhof potsdam stadt*

(P) The **Jewish cemetery** in Weissensee is one of the biggest in Europe, with more than 100,000 gravestones drawing a picture of the once-rich Jewish history in Berlin.
herbert-baum-strasse 45, weissensee, telephone 030 925 33 30, sun-thu 8am-4pm, s-bahnhof greifswalderstrasse

(Q) **Schloss Charlottenburg** is one of the few remaining castles in the city of Berlin. King Friedrich the 1st of Prussia built it in 1699 for his wife. It's considered to be the most pompous example of architecture under the Hohenzoller rule. The numerous historical rooms are overwhelmingly rich and boast rococo paintings and porcelain from the Far East. The surrounding park is also worth a visit, built in French baroque style.
spandauer damm, charlottenburg, telephone 030 32 09 11, open tue-fri 10am-5pm, admission € 12, u-bahnhof sophier-charlotte-platz

(R) The **Dorotheenstädtischer Friedhof** in Chausseestrasse is a beautiful cemetery where many famous German authors and intellectuals are buried. From Hegel to Wittgenstein, you'll see many familiar names in this cemetery, which is located close to the house where Bertolt Brecht used to live.
chausseestrasse, mitte, open tue-sat 10am-5pm, no admission, u-bahnhof oranienburger tor

(S) The **Strandbad Wannsee** in Zehlendorf is the most popular open-air bath in Berlin. In summer, half the city comes to this huge lake to relax on the 1.5 kilometer strip of beach. The Strandbad is a representative sample of Berlin's inhabitants - from Turkish muscle men and chic bikini-clad girls to beer-bellied fathers with families in tow, you'll see the full range of the city's people. There is a rental service for beach chairs and boats and also a small nudist strip.
wannseebadweg 25, zehlendorf, telephone 030 803 56 12, open daily from may 1st - august 31st, 10am-7pm, admission € 4, s-bahnhof nikolaissee

Nightlife

Berlin is most likely Europe's nightlife capital. There is no official curfew, which has allowed a very vivid nightlife culture to blossom over the last few decades. Film, dance, pop concerts, plays, theaters and clubs - the sky is the limit in Berlin. Have a look at bi-weekly magazines such as Tip or Zitty to see what's on where and when, or check out the English-language news-paper The Ex-Berliner, which has a wealth of practical information for non-German speaking tourists.

As the city with the most theaters in Germany, as well as three opera houses and two philharmonic orchestras, Berlin offers many attractions for high culture music fans as well as numerous theaters offering a wide range of performances. Musicals, however, are not very popular and it is not easy to find many theaters showing plays in English.

Cafés and bars are all open way past midnight. If you like to dance, definitely visit one of Berlin's famous clubs. From house to techno, electro to hip-hop, acid jazz to reggae, the Berlin club scene offers many choices. The above-mentioned magazines contain extensive listings of who's playing where, as well as what type of music it will be. Admission fees are fairly low compared to other European capitals, so a night of club hopping is a fairly common occasion amongst Berliners. You can find the letters on the overview map in the front of the book.

(T) **Tresor** is without a doubt Berlin's most famous techno club. Located in a former treasury, this is where international techno and house DJs spin from midnight till noon on weekends.
leipzigerstrasse 126a, telephone 030 229 06 11, open fri-sat midnight-noon, admission €10, u-bahnhof stadtmitte

(U) The **Watergate** opened recently and hosts a variety of excellent club nights, including local and international DJ talent. On Thursdays there's independent hip-hop, on Fridays drum 'n bass and on Saturdays deep house. The club's crowd is young and trendy and from the second floor, where there is a club with more of a lounge atmosphere, there is a great view over the Spree River.

falckensteinstrasse 49, telephone 030 61 28 03 94, www.water-gate.de, open thu-sat 11pm-whenever, admission €10, u-bahnhof görlitzer bahnhof

(V) The **WMF** is one of the most legendary clubs in Berlin and is particularly known because it's constantly moving. Now in its fifth location at Café Moskau, the club is open Thursday through Saturday and hosts everything electronic dance music can offer. On Fridays check out Berlin dj stars Jazzanova.

karl-marx-allee 34, mitte, telephone 03 288 78 89 10, www.wmfclub.de, open thu-sat 11pm-whenever, admission varies, u-bahnhof schillingstrasse

(W) The **Kaffe Burger** has nothing to do with burgers or coffee. Rather, it's a pub that looks very GDR-like from its interior. It hosts musical nights that range from country and rockabilly, to ska and sixties soul. At the very popular bi-monthly 'Russendisko', Russian music is played to a crowd drunk on vodka. The Kaffee Burger is very popular amongst theater people and literati.

torstrasse 60, mitte, telephone 030 28 04 64 95, www.kaffeeburger.de, open mon-thu from 9pm, fri-sat from 11pm, sun from 7pm, admission varies, u-bahnhof rosa-luxemburg-platz

(X) The **Roter Salon** at the Volksbühne Theater looks like a 1920s dancehall and is one of the few 'old school' dance spots that weren't erased during the war and GDR times. The music program is variable; from tango and salsa nights to indie rock parties and electronic concerts and readings, the Roter Salon is a spot where anything goes. The crowd is very mixed as well.
rosa-luxemburg-platz 2, mitte, telephone 030 24 06 58 06, www.roter-salon.de, open daily 8pm-whenever, admission varies, u-bahnhof rosa-luxemburg-platz

(Y) **A-Trane** is one of the main venues for jazz lovers in Berlin. From soul jazz to modern jazz, legends like Ray Brown, Herbie Hancock and Brad Mehldau have performed here, as well as local jazz talent, who come together for the Late Night Sessions every Saturday night. The crowd tends to be middle-aged and musically interested.
bleibtreustrasse1, charlottenburg, telephone 030 313 25 50, www.a-trane.de, open sun-thu 9pm-2am, fri-sat 9pm-open end, admission varies, u-bahnhof savignylplatz

Alphabetical index

Category index

food & drink

hotels

transportation

POTSDAM, SANS SOUCI

● **Sights**
● **Food & Drink**
● **Shopping**
○ **Nice to do**

Sights outside of the city center

If you follow the walks described in this guide, you will automatically pass most of Berlin's sights. But of course there's much more to do and see than one guide can cover. You can find more information on the website of the Berlin tourist board www.berlin.de or www.btm.de/english, where you can find information about the many museums and their collections, exhibitions, admission prices and opening hours. Some of the sights and areas that have not been covered in this guide's proposed walks, but that do deserve some special attention, are described below. You can find the letters on the overview map in the front of the book.

Ⓝ The **Karl Marx Allee** that leads from Mitte to Friedrichshain was built after World War II. Alongside the long and vast alley are houses built in 'Zuckerbäcker' style, an architectural style common in Eastern European countries under Soviet rule. It combines Russian constructivist architecture with neo-classicism. If you drive down Karl Marx Allee and the Frankfurter Tor you immediately get the impression that you are in an Eastern European city. When it was built, it was called Stalin-Allee; you'll see why.
karl marx allee, mitte and friedrichshain, u-bahnhof frankfurter tor

Ⓞ The **Flea Market** on the Strasse des 17.Juni, which leads from Tiergarten to Charlottenburg, is the biggest and most popular of Berlin's street markets. Here, private households as well as professionals sell antiques, arts & crafts, records, books and vintage clothing in good to excellent condition.
strasse des 17. juni, charlottenburg, telephone 030 26 55 00 96,
open sat-sun 10am-5pm, u-bahnhof ernst-reuter platz, s-bahnhof tiergarten

th the utmost care. Mo' Media BV cannot
naccuracies within the text. Any remarks or
the following address.

berlin, p.o. box 7028, 4800 ga, breda,
s, e-mail info@momedia.nl

man
a & simon jones
berger
ey
100procent.nl, naarden
afie, hendrik-ido-ambacht
ven & sasja lagendijk, mo' media
printing

7 117 4 - nur 510, 512
ia, breda, the netherlands, february 2004

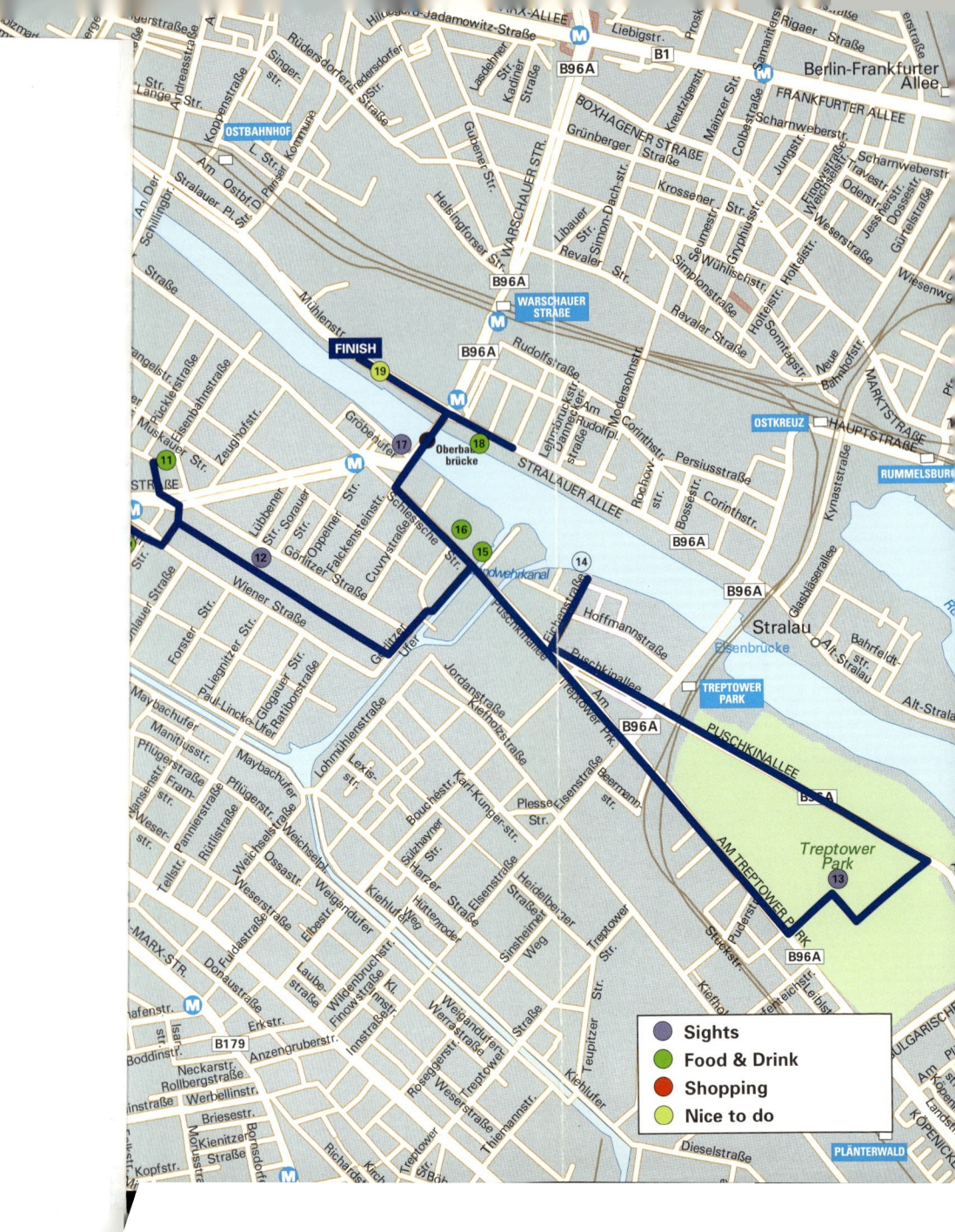

WWW.MOMEDIA.COM